GOOGLE

MW00900101

8 AND 8 PRO

USER GUIDE

The Step by Step Manual On How to Master Your Google Pixel 8 and 8 Pro For Beginners, Seniors, And Experts With Tips, Tricks, And Shortcuts, As Well As Visual Illustrations.

By

Richard S. Bryant

DISCLAIMER:

The information contained in this book is for educational purposes only. All efforts have been executed to present accurate, reliable, and up-to-date information contained herein. By reading this document, the reader agrees that under no circumstances is the author responsible for any losses, direct or indirect, which are incurred as a result of the information contained in this book including errors, omissions, and inaccuracy.

Table of Contents

INTRODUCTION

See the following graphic for a rundown of the functions available on your Pixel 8 Pro:

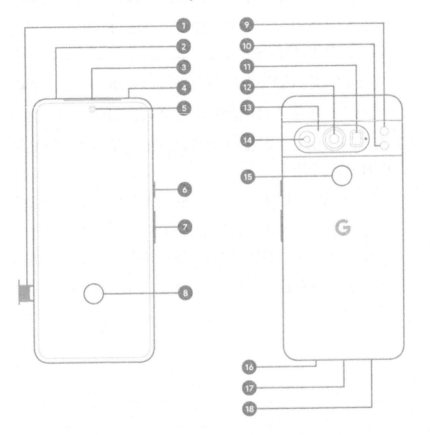

The Pixel 8 Pro's hardware components

See the following graphic for a rundown of the Pixel 8's capabilities:

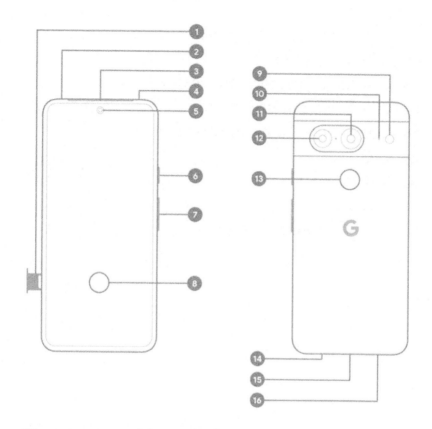

How to assemble a Pixel 8

1. Sim Card Tray
2. Mm Wave Antenna Cover
3. Top Speaker
4. Top Microphone
5. Front Facing Camera
6. Power Button
7. Volume up/down Button
8. Finger Print Sensor
9. Led Flash

10.   Temperature Sensor
11. 5x Telephoto Lens
12. Rear facing camera: ultrawide lens
13. Rear Facing Microphone
14. Rear Facing Camera: wide lens
15. NFC
16. Bottom Speaker
17. USB-C port
18.   Bottom Microphone

CHAPTER ONE

ASSEMBLE YOUR PIXEL WITH EASE

Depending on your needs, you may either transfer data from your old phone to your new Pixel phone or use your Pixel phone in its entirety.

- Most phones running Android 5.0 or later or iOS 8.0 or later can have their data transferred automatically.
- Data may be transferred manually from the majority of phones on the market.

USE YOUR EXISTING PHONE'S DATA TRANSFER CAPABILITY

Once your phone is turned on for the first time, follow the on-screen instructions to transfer data to it.

If you do not complete the initial setup or do not transmit data:

- You will get a message stating that the "Pixel setup isn't done" within a few minutes. To complete the setup, tap Finish.

- Keep the Settings app open for a few days. Click "Finish setup" in the upper right.
- Resetting your phone is an option you have at your disposal. You lose all of your info in the process.

Operating on an Android-powered mobile device

Before to beginning

1. Request a nano SIM card from your cellular provider if you do not already own one.
   eSIM may work with some Pixel phones; it all depends on the model and the service provider. Please contact your carrier for further information.
2. Look for a cord that is compatible with your present phone, such as the charging cord.
3. Locate your Quick Switch Adapter if your present device or cord does not have a USB-C port.

Move your information

When using an iPhone

Before beginning

1. Request a nano SIM card from your cellular provider if you do not already own one.

Word of advice: eSIM may work with some Pixel phones; it all depends on the model and the service provider.

2. Check that you can send and receive as much data as feasible.
3. Look for a cord that is compatible with your present phone, such as the charging cord.
4. Locate the Quick Switch Adapter.

Move your information

Accessible with Windows Phone or BlackBerry

Before beginning

Request a nano SIM card from your cellular provider if you do not already own one.

eSIM may work with some Pixel phones; it all depends on the model and the service provider. Please contact your carrier for further information.

Move your information

FORGET ABOUT DATA TRANSFERS

Just power on your Pixel phone hit the Start button, and then choose "Set up as new" if you're starting from scratch or if this is your first phone. You may begin customizing your new phone without ever having to transfer any data.

MOVE FROM AN ANDROID TO PIXEL

Acquire the Pixel by moving information from an Android device

Information such as texts, images, audio, calendar events, and applications may be copied.

Data transmission may be temporarily interrupted if your storage capacity is full, depending on your device. Before beginning data transmission, ensure that your storage capacity is sufficient.

THINGS THAT IS COMPATIBLE WITH THE PIXEL

The question of what copies are made during setup

All of your crucial data will be seamlessly transferred to Pixel.

Changing to Pixel won't need you to start from scratch. During setup, you may effortlessly transfer the following from your existing phone:

Applications and associated data (for applications shown in the Google Play store)

- Audio, visual, and moving images
- Accounts on Google
- Data kept by a SIM card or your mobile device

- Electronic messages
- Media files sent via SMS messaging
- Login information for mobile networks
- Different phones and versions of Android have different options.
- Desktop background Call log Alerts
- If you're using the same Google Account, you can access your passwords in Google Password Manager.
- Spotify and Fitbit are two examples of subscription services that you may access on your Pixel by logging into the respective apps.
- When you access your Google Account on your Pixel phone, you will see these:
- Contact information Events scheduled

Your Google Account information and anything else linked to it

Once the initial setup is complete, you may proceed to transmit the following:

- Data from accounts that aren't Google, such as contacts and calendar entries.
- Your LINE contacts and, if backed up, your entire chat history.
- Conversation history on WhatsApp.

The automated transfer of certain third-party applications and data is not guaranteed.

When setting up, what won't copy?

- Digital files, such as Portable Document Format (PDF) documents,
- Hidden or protected folders include media files such as photos, movies, and music.
- Applications not available in the Google Play Store
- Information retrieved from non-Android app backups
- Data associated with accounts that are not Google Accounts
- Synced calendars and contacts with providers other than Google
- Specific mobile device preferences (device and Android version dependent)

Data transfer Pixel 8 and Pixel 8 Pro users may transfer data.

Wireless data transmission is possible when you link your new Pixel phone with an Android device.

On the "Copy apps & data" screen, you should see an image. Press the image five times to switch to USB data transmission instead of Wi-Fi. Do this regardless of whether you have linked your phones or not.

Preparing the two phones for setup

Consider creating a Google Account if you haven't already. If you don't, your new Pixel phone won't be able to get app downloads and certain stuff won't transfer over.

As a first step, gather the following:

- Use your current, fully charged Android device running the most recent software.
- Comes with a brand-new Pixel phone that is fully charged.
- A reliable wireless network.
- If you want to utilize a real SIM card with your new Pixel, you'll need your SIM card and an insert tool.

Connect the two devices

1. Make sure both your old Android phone and the new Pixel phone are turned on.
2. Find the option to "Pixel" or "Android device" on the new Pixel phone.
3. Press the "Set up" button on the notice that appears on your current Android phone. It will bring up a QR code reader.

- Manually opening your Camera app is another option for scanning the QR code.
4. Scan the QR code with your old Android phone and then use your new Pixel phone to read it.

When you upgrade to a Pixel phone, your current Wi-Fi connection will follow you. Link your Pixel phone to a Wi-Fi network if your Android phone isn't already connected.

Get Your Pixel Phone Ready

1. Make sure your SIM is connected. You have the option to:
   - Get an eSIM card from your service provider. Carry out the download by following the on-screen instructions.
   - Get the SIM card or electronic SIM card onto your Google Pixel phone. Just follow the on-screen instructions to complete the transfer.
2. To unlock your Pixel phone, go to the settings menu on your old Android device.
   - Your Pixel phone will start to sync with your Google Accounts.
3. Configure the Face Unlock and Fingerprint Unlock features.

Make a copy of all of your Android device's data.

Step 2's phone pairing is required.

The on-screen prompts will guide you through selecting whatever data from your current Android smartphone to transfer. Apps, Google Accounts, and SMS messages are among the data types that may be transferred.

On the "Copy data from your Android device" page, you'll see an image. Press the picture five times to switch to USB data transfer instead of Wi-Fi. If you haven't linked your phones yet, you can still do this.

1. When prompted to "Copy data from your Android device," press the screen five times before selecting Next if you did not link your phone in Step 2.
2. Unlock your Android smartphone and turn it on.
3. To charge an Android smartphone, insert the charging cord into your device.
4. Place the other end into your Google Pixel phone.
   - Insert the Quick Switch Adapter into your Pixel phone if you happen to have one.
   - You can still transmit data wirelessly even if you don't have a charging cord.
5. Just go with the flow on your Android phone.
6. A catalog of your information shows up on your Pixel phone.

- Click Copy to copy all of your data.
- You may selectively copy data by disabling the options you don't want copied.

  Choose Copy.

7. Afterward, you will be able to use your phone.

   Be patient if it takes a while for an app to download and install.

If you want to restore from a cloud backup or do not have your previous device on hand,

1. Press Next on the "Copy data from your Android device" screen, which is located in the lower right corner.
2. In the "Restore data from an old device" prompt, locate and touch the device whose data you want to recover.
3. It shows a rundown of your information.
   - Select Restore to get back all of your information.
   - To get a subset of the data:

     To prevent restoring unwanted items, disable them.

     Select Restore.

4. You will be able to use your phone again after the repair is complete.

Seek assistance

For whatever assistance you may need, we are available at all times.

The Settings app is a good place to look for further instructions on how to configure your Pixel. After that, find Tips & support and touch on it.

Including Folder, moving data from Pixel 7 Pro and older models

1. The first thing you need to do is charge your new Pixel before you begin setting it up.
2. Make sure to install all the available updates on your existing phone.
3. Locate the necessary items.
   - An adapter that is compatible with your present phone, such as the charging cord.
   - If the port on your phone or cord isn't USB-C, you may use your Quick Switch Adapter.
   - Your SIM card and the device to insert it (unless you're using an eSIM and your cell provider is Google Fi).
4. When using a Pixel phone:

   Fire up your Google Pixel smartphone.

Using your Google

Start by powering up your Pixel. Your phone's language and vision settings are customizable.

Insert the SIM card

1. Stick your SIM card in.
2. A Start button will appear.

Link the mobile devices

To transfer information to a brand-new Pixel phone, you can use:

- Online data storage
- An old phone and a cord (ideal)
- Available over Wi-Fi (Android 12 and above)

Make a copy of your file.

Restore information with a cloud backup

1. When using a Pixel phone:
   - Press Start to begin setup.
   - Link up with your cell service provider or a Wi-Fi hotspot.
2. To proceed with the "Copy Apps & Data" prompt, choose Next.

3. "Use your old device" prompts you to tap. No longer compatible with previous-generation phones.
4. To access your Google Account backup, just follow the on-screen instructions.

USING A CABLE, TRANSFER DATA FROM YOUR PREVIOUS PHONE

1. When using a Pixel phone:
   - Press the beginning button.
   - Join a wireless network or your cell provider's network.
2. Then, when prompted to "Copy Apps & Data," Choose Next. Back up your information.
3. Scroll down to "Use your old device," and then press Next.
4. Unlock your Android smartphone and turn it on.
5. To charge an Android smartphone, insert the charging cord into your device.
6. Join your Pixel phone or the Quick Switch Adapter by inserting the opposite end of the cable into your device.

   No cable? No problem! You have the option to send and receive data wirelessly.

7. Find the Trust option on your Android handset.

8. A catalog of your information shows up on your Pixel phone.
   - Click Copy to copy all of your data.
   - You can selectively replicate data by disabling features you don't need.
   - Choose Copy.
   - Afterward, you will be able to use your phone.

Be patient if it takes a while for an app to download and install.

Wi-Fi data copying requires Android 12 or later.

Wi-Fi data transfers are only compatible with Android devices running versions 5 or later and 12 or later. Make sure both of your devices meet these requirements before trying to transmit data.

1. When using a Pixel phone:
   - Press the beginning button.
   - Join a wireless network or your cell provider's network.
2. Then, when prompted to "Copy Apps & Data," Choose Next. Back up your information.
3. Scroll down to "Use your old device," and then press Next.
4. Choose "No cable?" when prompted to locate the cord for your previous phone.

5. Find the alert and hit the "Ok" button.
6. Get your present phone started and unlocked.
7. To begin setting up your new phone, open the notification on your existing phone.
8. A catalog of your information will be accessible on your Pixel phone.
   - Click Copy to copy all of your data.
   - You can selectively replicate data by disabling features you don't need.
   - Choose Copy.
9. You will be able to use your phone after the transfer is complete.

MOVE FROM AN IPHONE TO PIXEL DEVICES

You can transfer everything of your information from an iPhone to a Pixel phone, including messages, images, music, contacts, applications, and calendars.

Data transmission may be temporarily interrupted if your storage capacity is full, depending on your device. Before beginning data transmission, ensure that your storage capacity is sufficient.

THINGS THAT IS COMPATIBLE WITH THE PIXEL

While preparing, what copies

All of your crucial data will be seamlessly transferred to Pixel.

You won't have to start from scratch when you upgrade from iPhone® to Pixel. The following are only some of the things that are easily transferable1 from your current phone to Pixel:

Data Type	Cable	WiFi
Phone and iCloud contacts and calendars	Yes	Yes
Photos and videos saved on your iPhone	Yes	Yes
Texts, iMessages, and most iMessage content, like photos, videos, and other media	Yes	No
WhatsApp chat history	Yes	No
Free apps (if the Android version is available on Google Play)	Yes	No
Music (MP3s and audio files)	Yes	No
Notes	Yes	No
Wallpapers that use your photos, but not standard ones included with your phone	Yes	No
Call history: Transfers if the device is set up to encrypt local backup.	Yes	No
Home screen layout	Yes	No

After initial setup, here's what else you can transfer over:

Data Type	Cable	WiFi
Music: your music from subscription services such as Spotify or Apple Music (just sign into the service on your Pixel)	Yes	Yes
Non-Google accounts and their data, including contacts and calendar events (just sign into the service on your Pixel)	Yes	Yes
Passwords from Google Password Manager (if you use the same Google Account)	Yes	Yes
LINE contacts and 2 weeks of chat conversations.	Yes	Yes
Progress that you have made in some gaming apps or websites (just sign in on your Pixel)	Yes	Yes
Photos, videos, documents, and other files stored in iCloud with a transfer of your iCloud photos and videos to Google Photos. As an alternative, sign in to icloud.com on your computer, choose the files you want, export them, and then upload them to Google Photos (for photos and videos) and Google Drive (for miscellaneous files and PDFs). Based on your library size, it might take several hours or days, and may require purchase of a Google One storage plan.	Yes	Yes

Not all third-party applications and data will be immediately migrated.

All of your copied Google contacts, calendars, and Keep notes will sync with your Pixel phone and your online Google Account. By logging into your Google Account on your Pixel phone, all of your Google Account information is synced.

Uncopyable items during setup

- Paid via the app
- Device preferences, such as Wi-Fi security codes
- Protection for musical works with Digital Rights Management (DRM)
- Safari® Favorites
- Expensed applications and those not listed on Google Play
- Certain app data, such as app data not kept on the cloud

TRACK DOWN THE NECESSARY ITEMS

1. An Adapter for the Rapid Switch
2. A Lightning connector, similar to the one you use to charge your iPhone
3. Unless you're using an eSIM, your SIM card and the equipment to insert it

TURN ON YOUR IPHONE

- Do not use FaceTime or iMessage.
- Your ability to send data may be restricted if your iPhone is in the possession of an institution such as a school or workplace.

Data transmission to Pixel is not supported on iOS beta versions.

USING YOUR PIXEL

Start by powering up your Pixel. The language and vision settings on your phone are customizable.

CONFIGURE USING AN ALTERNATE DEVICE

The Pixel 8 and Pixel Pro are the only devices that need this step.

1. On the Pixel handset:
   - Touch the screen of your iOS device.

Go online to your Google account over a mobile network or Wi-Fi.

The sequence of displays could change depending on the connection, and this process is exclusive to the Pixel 8 and Pixel Pro.

1. Get online by joining a Wi-Fi network or, failing that, by inserting a SIM card and joining your mobile network.
2. Access your Google Account by signing in.
   - One thing you need is a Google Account. Otherwise, you won't be able to transfer some files to your new smartphone and won't be able to download programs.

3. Get your eSIM card downloaded so you may join a mobile network. To insert your SIM card, follow the on-screen instructions otherwise.

Your Pixel may use an eSIM card from any cell provider. To find out more information, contact your carrier.

CHOOSE AN UNLOCK METHOD FOR YOUR DEVICE

Just make sure you have a Pixel 8 or Pixel 8 Pro before you go.

- Retrieve Passwords by Fingerprint
- Enable Face Unlock,

LINK THE PHONES AND TRANSFER THE INFO

1. Launch the app on your Pixel phone.
2. Join a wireless network or your cell provider's network.
3. After being prompted to "Copy data from your iPhone or iPad," choose Next. Back up your information.
4. When prompted to "Use your old device," choose Next.
5. Unlock your iPhone and turn it on.
6. To charge your iPhone, insert one end of the charging cord into your device.

7. Connect either your Pixel phone or the Quick Switch Adapter to the opposite end of the cord.
   - No cable? No problem! While wireless data transfers are possible, the vast majority of data types are better sent via cable.
8. On the iPhone, choose Trust.
9. A rundown of all the data kinds you have on your Pixel phone will show up.
   - System files and connected iCloud data might cause the storage capacity of your iPhone to trigger a capacity alert. Ignore the warning and proceed if you are certain that all of the data stored on your device can be transferred. Using an iPhone You can see the amount of storage space being utilized by tapping on Settings, then General, and finally iPhone Storage.
   - If you want to copy everything, just hit Copy.
   - To selectively copy data, just uncheck the boxes that correspond to the things you do not want copied.

   Press the Copy button.

10. While the Pixel is being transferred, you may keep on configuring it.

11. You may check the results and get advice on how to transfer any missing material by reviewing the screens that provide the transfer summary once the transfer is finished.

12. On your iPhone, toggle off iMessage.
   - A popup will appear to prompt you to disable iMessage. You should be good to go if you finish this before setup. Do it immediately if you haven't already.
   - Some text messages may not arrive on your new Pixel smartphone unless you disable iMessage.

13. Not required: Migrate your data stored in iCloud.
   - You can only use a cable to transmit data stored on your device. To ensure that data stored in iCloud or other cloud services is accessible on your Pixel, follow the on-screen instructions.

Your applications may take some time to display once the transfer is complete since they have to download and install.

CHAPTER TWO

REPLACE IMESSAGE WITH GOOGLE MESSAGES

Transfer your text messages from Apple's iMessage to Android's Messages on your brand-new Android phone.

Take your iPhone's SIM card out first

Before you take the SIM card out of your iPhone, make sure iMessage is disabled. In any other case, your new phone may keep receiving SMS and MMS messages from your previous iPhone.

Activate iMessage

1. Access the Settings menu on your iPhone.
2. Press on Messages.
3. Put iMessage on "Off" mode.

Turn off group conversations.

Create a new group chat if you're already in one with friends who have iPhones; that way, you'll always be able to receive their messages. The new group chat is open to all of your friends as well.

Has your iPhone's SIM card already been removed?

If you've already taken the SIM card out of your previous iPhone or don't have it on hand, you may ask Apple to deregister your number using iMessage.

CHARGE YOUR PIXEL PHONE BATTERIES

With a USB-C connection, you can charge any Pixel phone. Some phones, like the Pixel 5a (5G), come with a power adaptor that you should utilize for optimal performance.

Wirelessly charge Qi-certified devices and accessories via Battery Share. This includes Pixel Buds and Pixel 5-7 Pro (except 6a and 7a). Place your phone's back onto an accessory or other device to charge it.

As your Pixel phone ages, its battery life may decrease as a result of factors including temperature, use habits, and general wear and tear. Some Pixel phones can automatically modify charging settings to control device and battery temperatures, which may assist in saving battery life. This may cause the charging speed to decrease in some instances.

Remember to keep your phone's battery fully charged to use Battery Share for wireless charging. Launch the Settings app on your phone to see the current battery life. Select Battery, followed by Battery Share. Locate your phone in an area where it will not grow very heated.

HOW TO CHARGE YOUR PIXEL PHONE

1. Attach the USB-C cable to your phone by inserting both ends into the connector located on the base.
2. Connect the other end of the cord to your phone's power adapter.
3. Connect your power adapter to an electrical socket.

USE ADAPTIVE CHARGING

A feature called Adaptive Charging may activate an hour before you disconnect from a lengthy or overnight charging session, bringing the battery life of your phone to 100%. An improved battery life is yours to enjoy with the Adaptive Charging function. The following phones are compatible with the feature:

- When you charge your Pixel 4 from 9 PM to 4 AM and have an alarm set for 3-10 AM, it will turn on.
- The latest Pixel devices include Fold: Your charging patterns are learned via the Adaptive Charging function. It may still activate even if none of the aforementioned parameters are met if a lengthy charging session is anticipated.

This function takes around 14 days to understand how you typically charge your device. Adaptive Charging cannot activate if your charging patterns change, such as while you're on the road.

Stop Adaptive Charging by doing:

1. Go to the Settings app on your phone.
2. Select Adaptive Charging from the Battery menu.
3. Disable the Adaptive Charging feature.

When you enable Adaptive Charging, a notice will show up that tells you when your battery will be completely charged.

ADVICE ON CHARGING
Methods for swiftly charging

- To charge, plug it into an electrical socket. Laptops and other portable electronics might charge at a slower rate.
- While your phone charges, you may use it. Put it away while it charges for quicker charging.

Find out when your phone needs a charge

1. Turn on the ring tone for your phone.
2. Go to the Settings app on your phone.
3. Choose Sound, and then go to Advanced.
4. Hide the charging noises.
5. There will be a sound when you connect your phone to the charger.

   No sound will be audible if your phone is silenced or set to vibrate.

Which power cords and adapters are best?

- Charge your Pixel phone using a USB-C cord and a USB 2.0 power converter.
- Use a USB-C to USB-A cable to charge your phone with a USB-A power adapter. Compared to USB-C, this method of charging your phone is slower.
- Use a power adapter with a rating of 30 W or above, such as the Google 30 W USB-C adapter, or any other PPS adapter. You could also try

using an additional USB Power Delivery (PD) adapter with a 15 W rating.

- Pixel phones may not be compatible with other Android cords or power adapters.
- Wireless charging is not compatible with the Pixel 4a (5G), Pixel 4a, Pixel 3a, Pixel 2, or Pixel (2016) smartphones.

Make sure your gadget can charge your phone before you use it.

Your phone may not be compatible with the cable or USB power adapter you're using, or it might be broken, if you power on your phone but a "Check charging accessory" message appears. Your phone will charge very slowly, if it charges at all, according to this. To resolve the issue, try charging with an alternate cable and a PPS adapter with a power rating of 30 W or more, or a PD adapter with a rating of 15 W or higher.

Technical details

- We advise taking it to an authorized repair service provider if you want to remove the battery. Do not attempt to remove it by yourself; we advise against it.
- Each nation or area has its power adaptor.

Is your Pixel phone still giving you trouble?

Post your query on our forums and the Pixel community will respond with potential answers to any problems you may be experiencing with your phone's reset.

POWER ON/ OFF YOUR PIXEL PHONE

The top button on the right side of your phone is where you may switch it on and off.

ENABLE OR DISABLE YOUR POWER

- When your phone is turned off, you may switch it back on by pressing and holding the Power button for a few seconds.
- Press and hold the Power button on Pixel 6 and subsequent devices until you hear a beep, which could take up to seven seconds in certain cases.
- Turning off your phone when it's on:
- Keep the Power button pressed down for a few seconds on Pixel 5a and older models. Next, choose Power off Power from the screen.
- Holding down the Power and volume up keys for a few seconds turns off your phone on Pixel 6 and subsequent models. Next, choose Power off Power from the screen.
  Charge your phone before using it.

TOGGLE THE SCREEN'S POWER ON AND OFF

Pressing the Power button once toggles the screen's on/off functionality when the phone is powered on.

Even when you turn off your screen, certain Pixel phones display the clock and other information.

BOOT UP AGAIN

1. Start your phone up again.
    *   Pixel 5a and previous models: Hold the power button down for 30 seconds, or until your phone turns off and then turns back on.
    *   For Pixel 6 and subsequent models, alongside Fold: For a few seconds, press and hold the Power button and the Volume up button.
2. Click on Restart.

TOP UP YOUR PIXEL PHONE WITH A SIM CARD

If your phone's nano SIM or eSIM is activated, you may link it to a mobile network. If you don't have one, a notification saying "No SIM card" will appear.

Some of these instructions are only compatible with Android 11 and later.

The Pixel 8 and subsequent phones do not support all previous SIM cards. You will get the notice "This

SIM is no longer supported" if you try to use a SIM card that isn't compatible. "Get a new SIM" by contacting your carrier.

HOW TO USE A SIM CARD

You may use nano SIM cards with any Pixel phone. One more thing: eSIM is compatible with certain Pixel phones.

While shopping for a Pixel phone from Google:

- In the US, you have the option to either not use a SIM card or have one pre-inserted by Verizon. To activate your SIM card with Verizon, visit their website.
- There is no SIM card included with your phone for use in other countries.

Go for a tiny SIM slot

- Get in touch with your cellular operator to get a nano SIM card.
- Transferring the nano SIM card from another phone to your present one is an alternative to purchasing a new one.

Employ eSIM

Depending on the phone and cell provider, eSIM may be used by certain phones. To find out more information, contact your carrier.

- Everything from the Pixel 4 onwards is compatible with eSIM.
- Phones purchased in Japan or with Verizon service do not support eSIM, including the Pixel 3a.
- Pixel 3: eSIM is incompatible with phones purchased with service from any US or Canadian carrier save Sprint and Google Fi. There are a few more countries where eSIM won't work: Japan, Taiwan, and Australia.
- Pixel 2: eSIM is only compatible with phones purchased with Google Fi.
- No phones are compatible with eSIM as of Pixel (2016).

INSERT A SIM CARD

While the phone is turned off, insert a SIM card:

1. The SIM ejection tool is located in a tiny hole on the left side of the phone.
   - The SIM card slot may be found on the bottom side of the Pixel 3 (2018).
2. To remove the tray, gently yet firmly press on it.

3. Place the nano SIM card into the tray after removing it.
4. Return the tray to its place by gently pushing it in.

To restore cell service, you may have to power cycle your phone. Holding down the power button for about three seconds will restart an active phone. Select Restart.

Place the SIM card on the phone.

LOCATE THE UNIQUE IDENTIFIERS FOR YOUR PHONE

Pixel ID numbers such as the IMEI 1, IMEI 2, or EID may be required while communicating with your carrier.

LINK YOUR PIXEL TO WIRELESS NETWORKS

You may customize your Wi-Fi experience by adjusting the time and method your device connects.

Your device will automatically connect to neighboring Wi-Fi networks that you have previously connected to when you switch on Wi-Fi. Your smartphone now has the option to activate Wi-Fi automatically when it detects networks that you have stored.

Some of these instructions are only compatible with Android 11 and later.

POWER UP AND LINK UP

1. Launch the Settings app on your smartphone.
2. Press on Network & internet, followed by Internet.
3. Enable the Wi-Fi.
4. Press on one of the available networks. The Lock will be shown if a password is required. "Connected" will appear under the network name after you've connected.
   - Your network has been "Saved." The connection is established automatically

whenever your device is in range and has Wi-Fi enabled.

As an additional tip, you may access your Wi-Fi settings by swiping down on your screen.

Get in touch via push alert

Enabling Wi-Fi enables the ability to get alerts about nearby, high-quality public networks. Regarding these alerts:

- Tap Connect to establish a connection to the network.
- Select All Networks to see the Wi-Fi options menu.
- Just clear the notice to stop receiving alerts for that network.

You have the option to connect to these networks discreetly as well.

Evaluate different network strengths

Strength

1. Go to the Settings app on your phone.
2. Press on Network & internet, followed by Internet.
3. Verify that the Wi-Fi is turned on.

4. The Wi-Fi symbol will show you the strength of the network's signal. A more robust symbol signifies a more robust signal.

Speed

1. Go to the Settings app on your phone.
2. Press on Network & internet, followed by Internet.
3. Verify that the Wi-Fi is turned on.
4. The name of a public network is where you may discover the connection speed. As the signal strength changes, so may the speed.
   - You can send and receive SMS and emails, but it's slow. Slowly, images will load.
   - OK: Web browsing, social networking, and streaming of music and SD videos are all within your capabilities.
   - Quick: You can make video calls and stream most HD videos.
   - Quick: You can watch movies of excellent quality online.

Turn on when you're close to your saved networks

1. Go to the Settings app on your phone.
2. To access your network settings, go to Network & internet, then tap Internet.

3. Switch on automatically enable Wi-Fi. To enable Location and Location services, you must first turn them on.
4. Enable the scanning of Wi-Fi and Bluetooth.

Wi-Fi will not activate immediately if you do:

- I am sorry, but the location is incorrect.
- This device's power-saving mode is active.
- Turn on the airplane mode.
- Background activity involving tethering (or "hotspot") Wi-Fi detection is disabled.

EDIT, ADD, SHARE, AND DELETE STORED NETWORKS

Modify an existing network

1. Go to the Settings app on your phone.
2. Choose "Network & internet" Next, we have Wi-Fi.
   - Select a network name to switch between them.
   - Pressing on a network will bring up its settings.

Include a previously saved web

PERMIT THE NETWORK LIST TO REFRESH

Just wait for the list to refresh if the network you're looking for isn't shown, but it's close by.

INTEGRATE NETWORK

1. Go to the Settings app on your phone.
2. Press on Network & internet, followed by Internet.
3. Verify that the Wi-Fi is turned on.
4. Select "Add network" from the list's bottom.
5. If prompted, provide the SSID and other security information for the network.
6. Hit the Save button.

Give a buddy your Wi-Fi password

1. Go to the Settings app on your phone.
2. Press on Network & internet, followed by Internet.
3. Verify that the Wi-Fi is turned on.
4. Go to Share after tapping on a network.
5. A QR code may be found on your mobile device. Scan the code and your buddy may join the same network.

Deleting a previously stored network

1. Go to the Settings app on your phone.

2. Press on Network & internet, followed by Internet.
3. Verify that the Wi-Fi is turned on.
4. Tap and hold a network that you've saved.
5. Select the "Forget" option.

ACCESS OPEN ROAMING WIRELESS NETWORKS

Wi-Fi hotspots form a federation called OpenRoaming. Your Google Pixel phone may automatically connect to OpenRoaming hotspots when you're in range, providing safe, no-cost internet access to other Google users.

Configure OpenRoaming

You must be within range of an OpenRoaming network to configure OpenRoaming. Your phone will immediately begin connecting to any nearby OpenRoaming networks after you've finished setting it up.

For Google Pixel users, to enable OpenRoaming:

1. Go to the Settings app on your phone.
2. Press on Network & internet, followed by Internet.
3. Select an OpenRoaming network from the available Wi-Fi networks.

4. See the T&Cs shown on the screen. Press the Continue button.
5. Select your Google account and tap the "Auth" button.

Disable or modify the OpenRoaming configuration.

The OpenRoaming account you use might be changed, forgotten, or disconnected.

1. Get into your phone's settings when it's linked to an OpenRoaming hotspot.
2. Press on Network & internet, followed by Internet.
3. See "OpenRoaming" and then press Settings.
   - Use the "Disconnect" button to end your connection to that particular hotspot.
   - Press the Forget button to permanently disconnect from OpenRoaming.
   - Go to the OpenRoaming settings menu, then tap on Advanced, and finally, Subscription, to modify your account.

You may find further information, including the frequency, security, and signal strength of the current hotspot, under the Settings menu.

Functionality of OpenRoaming

Google will not share any information about you with OpenRoaming networks.

The OpenRoaming feature streamlines the process of connecting to public Wi-Fi hotspots. You won't need to manually accept new terms and conditions when you go between networks. On the contrary, if you go from one section of a hotspot to another, your Pixel phone will automatically switch networks.

Networks are required to adhere to service and security criteria as well as agree to common terms and conditions to become members of OpenRoaming. When you set up OpenRoaming, you accept those standard conditions once.

Once that is done, your Pixel phone may use a Google credential to connect to OpenRoaming networks. This credential verifies that the account your phone is linked to has agreed to the rules. Your Pixel phone can now seamlessly transition between OpenRoaming hotspots thanks to this.

LINK A PIXEL PHONE TO CELLULAR DATA PLANS

To modify your phone's data use, go into the mobile network settings.

Automatically connecting to your carrier's fastest available data network is something that may be configured in your service plan. You may also have to configure your device for a certain carrier or insert a SIM card.

5G service is compatible with phones released after the Pixel 4a (5G).

Some of these instructions are only compatible with Android 11 and later.

UPDATE THE MOBILE NETWORK'S CONFIGURATION

1. Go to the Settings app on your phone.
2. First, go to Network & internet. Then, choose SIMs.
3. Press on a configuration option.

Hit System and then Reset options in your phone's Settings app to erase all of your network settings. Pick Reset from the Mobile Network Settings.

Options for mobile network configuration

Each phone and version of Android has its own unique set of options:

- Activate or deactivate mobile data.
- Allow your phone to use data networks other than your carrier's while you're outside of their service region (also known as "roaming").
- Use of app data
- Data restriction and warning
- Network type that is preferred: From choices like 5G and LTE, choose the network type that best suits your needs.
- Network: Find a network operator that suits your needs.
- Keys to the access point: Facilitate the secure connection of your phone by assisting your carrier in determining the correct IP address.

Settings for mobile networks and multiple SIM cards

Utilize the tabs located at the top of "Mobile network settings." If your phone is equipped with several SIM cards, you may modify the mobile network information for each SIM card individually.

Change the SIM card that is used for all of your phone calls, texts, and data.

1. Go to your device's settings.
2. To access your network, go to Network & internet, then choose SIMs.
3. Personalize each network according to your liking:
   - Data: Get the mobile data going.

     The default data SIM may only be one SIM. You will be notified if one is already in place.

   - Select "Call Preference" from the menu that appears. The next step is to choose your default carriers or to always ask.
   - Choose "SMS Preference" from the menu that appears inside the text message. The next step is to choose your default carriers or to always ask.

Make calls using a separate SIM card.

During a call, you will not be able to receive a call on the other SIM card. Via voicemail will go through any calls made to the second SIM card.

When transmitting data, the default SIM card for that use case is used most of the time. With one notable exception: All information sent on a phone call passes via the SIM card used to make the call.

Using a SIM card that isn't often utilized for data during calls:

1. Go to your device's settings.
2. Press on Network & internet, followed by SIMs.
3. Activate data while on the phone.

GET YOUR MOBILE NETWORK BACK UP

Network throughput and speed are not constant. Your network's kind, traffic, and distance from its antennas are all factors to consider.

Follow these procedures to fix a poor or nonexistent connection, even if you're inside your network's service area:

Verify settings, updates, and mistakes

1. Talk to your service provider if you get a SIM-related problem message.
   - An error message stating "Voice unavailable" or "Voice interruptions" might appear if you use two SIM cards.
2. Verify that Airplane Mode is not enabled.
   - Go to the Settings app on your phone.
   - Select Network and Internet.
   - Remove the Airplane mode setting.
3. Clear all of your network settings.
   - Go to the Settings app on your phone.

- Select Reset settings from the System menu.
- Choose Reset Mobile Network Settings.

4. Please ensure that you have installed any necessary system updates.

Before you buy a SIM card, be sure it is compatible with your phone and network.

Verify sluggish 5G connection.

When you're in a 5G service region, your phone will display a 5G symbol in the status bar. At that moment, it doesn't imply that your phone is receiving 5G service.

Give them a go:

- Exit Battery Saver mode. Enabling Battery Saver disables 5G.
- 5G service is available in less extensive regions than existing carrier networks. Find out what areas your carrier covers with 5G by contacting them.
- A variety of 5G options may be made available by various carrier networks. The speeds might be different. To find out what kind and how fast your 5G is, contact your carrier.
- Mobile service, especially 5G, may be disrupted by signal barriers such as buildings, walls, and

certain phone cases. Seek out ways to sidestep or eliminate obstacles.

- When 5G isn't an option, Pixel phones equipped with 5G will revert to using 4G or lesser networks.

Make sure it's compatible with 5G

All major carriers are compatible with Pixel phones. However, not all 5G networks are compatible with Pixel 4a and subsequent phones. Verify with your service provider that your handset is compatible with their 5G network.

The kind of 5G service you need is dependent on both your phone's model and the network your carrier uses. In the United States, Verizon has its own exclusive Pixel 4a (5G) phone.

Validate for system updates (exclusive to Denmark, Norway, and Sweden)

- Problems connecting Pixel to 5G network or any connection difficulties at all
- To those who own a Pixel 6a, 7, or 7 Pro and who use the networks of TDC in Denmark or ICE in Norway
- Get the most recent software update for your phone if you want to use the 5G network.

- To apply the patch:
- Launch System Update by navigating to Settings > System.
- Updates to the Pixel 7 and 7 Pro: When you set up your phone, you'll see an option to apply the system update.
- For users of the OneCall and MyCall (Norway) networks who own Pixel devices
- The availability of 5G services varies by country and may not be compatible with all carrier networks.
- Performance, speed, and 5G service could be affected by the capabilities of the operator's network and the intensity of the signal. Results can differ in practice. Not every place supports every function. Rates for data transfer could be different.
- My Pixel won't connect to Wi-Fi calls The capabilities of Wi-Fi calling differ from one nation to another, and they may not operate with every network provider. A lot of things affect how well and how high-quality calls work. The capabilities of the Wi-Fi network and the intensity of the signal are two of these criteria.

USE ALL THE MAJOR MOBILE NETWORKS

The Pixel phone is compatible with all major mobile networks.

Unlocking a phone's SIM card allows you to use it with any network, not simply the one the vendor has set up. Whether your phone is SIM-locked or not depends on where you purchased it.

All major carriers are compatible with Pixel phones. However, not all 5G networks are compatible with Pixel 4a and subsequent phones. Verify with your service provider that your handset is compatible with their 5G network.

A SIM-UNLOCKED PHONE IS A GOOD INVESTMENT

Any cell service provider may utilize your Pixel if your phone is SIM-unlocked. You may buy phones from the Google Store with no network lock.

To activate a SIM-free phone:

1. Purchase an unlocked Pixel handset from the official Google Store.
2. To reach your cell provider, dial *56.
3. To activate your phone for their service plan, follow their on-screen instructions.

Unlocked phones bought from the Google Play Store will show "Fi" until you connect them to your carrier.

If your phone is SIM-locked

A phone purchased from a cellular operator may be SIM-locked for two years. In such case, the phone will be unable to use any other carrier's mobile network until either the seller unlocks it or the contract expires.

Before your sales contract expires, you may contact your mobile service provider to explore the possibility of removing the SIM lock from your phone.

RESOLVE CONCERNS RELATED TO A SIM-LOCK FAILURE

After your previous carrier unlocked your SIM and your new provider verified your service, you may need to reset your SIM status if your replacement SIM still doesn't function. A message such as "Your service can't be activated" or "SIM card isn't supported" may appear.

Use simple procedures to fix problems

1. Find a Wi-Fi hotspot.
2. After an Android update, install it.

3. Launch the app on your phone.
4. Press the following code: 7465625.
5. Hold on for about two minutes after your phone goes back to the dialer screen.
6. Verify that a mobile network is available.

Perform advanced troubleshooting procedures

Do a factory reset.

Resetting your phone to its factory settings is an option to consider if basic troubleshooting fails to resolve the problem.

After wiping all data from your phone, you may set it up by selecting the restart option and then following the on-screen instructions.

Get in touch with your wireless provider.

If getting back to factory settings doesn't fix the problem of your phone not connecting to the mobile network, then you should contact your carrier.

CHAPTER THREE

HOW TO UTILIZE TWO SIM CARDS AT ONCE

Two SIM cards, one physical and one electronic, may be used with a Pixel 3a or later Pixel phone. When you make a call or send a message, you may choose which SIM to use. Dual SIM Dual Standby refers to this feature.

If your carrier permits it, you may utilize two eSim profiles concurrently on Pixel 7/7 Pro and subsequent smartphones.

You must insert the first SIM card before you may insert the second.

For some cell providers, DSDS and eSIM are compatible. Check with your cell provider to see whether they are compatible with your phone. Your Pixel 3a cannot have two SIM cards if you purchased it in Japan.

Dual SIM phones, such as the Pixel 4a (5G), and subsequent models can connect to 5G networks.

Some of these instructions are only compatible with Android 11 and later.

Use an eSIM to add a second SIM card.

For phones that do not yet have an eSIM but are utilizing a SIM card:

1. Go to the Settings app on your phone.
2. Press on Network & internet.
3. Find "Mobile network" and then press the "Add" button.
4. Would you want to download a SIM instead?
5. If prompted to "Use 2 SIMs?" then choose Yes. It will refresh on your phone.
6. Go back into your phone's Settings after an update.
7. Navigate to the Mobile network by tapping on Network & internet.
8. To customize your call and text settings, just touch on your networks.

You may set your phone to always ask for your network option by tapping the "Ask me every time" button.

Set up two eSim accounts.

You may activate two eSim profiles on a device that qualifies:

1. Go to the Settings app on your phone.
2. Select SIMs from the Network & Internet menu.

3. Tap Want to use a SIM card instead?
4. Pay attention to the directions.

Install a second SIM card

When utilizing an eSIM on a phone that does not yet have a SIM card:

1. Please insert the SIM card.
2. If prompted to "Use 2 SIMs?" then choose Yes. It will refresh on your phone.
3. Go back into your phone's Settings after an update.
4. Navigate to the Mobile network by tapping on Network & internet.
5. To customize your call and text settings, just touch on your networks.

You may set your phone to always ask for your network option by tapping the "Ask me every time" button.

CUSTOMIZE YOUR PHONE'S MULTI SIM SETTINGS

Some of these instructions are only compatible with Android 11 and later.

Different SIM cards may be used for different functions on your phone, such as data, calls, texts, and more. By default, your phone will utilize that SIM card.

Change the SIM card that is used for all of your phone calls, texts, and data.

1. Go to your device's settings.
2. To access your network, go to Network & internet, then choose SIMs.
3. Personalize each network according to your liking:
   - Data: Get the mobile data going.
     The default data SIM may only be one SIM. You will be notified if one is already in place.
   - Select "Call Preference" from the menu that appears. The next step is to choose your default carriers or to always ask.
   - Choose "SMS Preference" from the menu that appears inside the text message. The next step is to choose your default carriers or to always ask.

Make calls using a separate SIM card.

During a call, you will not be able to receive a call on the other SIM card. Via voicemail will go through any calls made to the second SIM card.

When transmitting data, the default SIM card for that use case is used most of the time. With one notable exception: All information sent on a phone call passes via the SIM card used to make the call.

Using a SIM card that isn't often utilized for data during calls:

1. Go to your device's settings.
2. Press on Network & internet, followed by SIMs.
3. Activate data while on the phone.

REMOVING OR CEASING USE OF A SIM

Some of these instructions are only compatible with Android 11 and later.

Temporarily disable a SIM

To briefly disable a SIM:

1. Go to the Settings app on your phone.
2. Navigate to the Mobile network by tapping on Network & internet.
3. To deactivate a SIM card, choose it.
4. Touch the "Use SIM" button.

Your phone can connect to 5G networks if it is in dual SIM mode or later, including the Pixel 4a (5G).

Remove an eSIM or make it password-protected

Get rid of an eSIM

1. Go to the Settings app on your phone.
2. Navigate to the Mobile network by tapping on Network & internet.
3. Choose the eSIM that you want to remove.
4. Hit the "Delete SIM" button.

Deleting an eSIM requires a password.

1. Go to the Settings app on your phone.
2. Select Advanced from the Security menu, and finally, Confirm SIM erasure.
3. Put down the SIM card

Detach it from the mobile device.

Resolve issues related to dual SIMs

Some of these instructions are only compatible with Android 11 and later.

Not all SIM card combinations are compatible with one another. "Voice unavailable" or "Voice interruptions" notifications indicate that your two SIMs' networks aren't communicating well with each other. Reach out to your cellphone provider for assistance.

LOCATE THE UNIQUE IDENTIFIERS FOR YOUR PHONE

Pixel ID numbers such as the IMEI 1, IMEI 2, or EID may be required while communicating with your carrier.

PERSONALIZE THE BACKGROUND OF YOUR PHONE

The home screen and lock screen backgrounds on your phone are customizable. Pick from your picture library or use the default photographs on your phone, even ones that update them.

- Android 10 and later are required to complete some of these procedures.
- Touching the screen is necessary for some of these procedures.

Customize your background

1. Locate an empty area on your phone's home screen by touching and holding it.
2. Select Wallpaper and style. For those who don't see "Wallpaper & style," just touch on Wallpapers.
3. Press on Reset Wallpaper.
   - Select "My photos" to upload a picture of your own.

- Select a category, then a picture, to use a curated one.
- Pixel 2 and onwards: After selecting Bloom or Living Universe, choose a wallpaper to utilize as a live background. To download, press the button.
- Just for Pixel 4 users: Before you can use Motion Sense to interact with your wallpaper, you need to set up Live Wallpaper. Select a wallpaper by tapping on Come Alive, and then tap Download.

4. Click "Done" or "Set wallpaper" at the very bottom.
5. Deciding which screen(s) to display the wallpaper on is an option if given.

Customize your picture wallpapers with effects (Pixel 6 and later)

1. Locate an empty area on your phone's home screen by touching and holding it.
2. Press on Wallpaper, and then choose My pictures.
3. Pick a picture.
4. Click on Effects.
5. To make a cinematic wallpaper, turn it on.
6. Select the Lock screen from the Home screen to preview your wallpaper.

7. Use the Home screen, Lock screen, or both screens to choose where to set your wallpaper.

Make your home screen backgrounds (Pixel 4a and later)

1. Pick an emoji or get a mixed bag:
   - Locate an empty area on your phone's home screen by touching and holding it.
   - Select "Wallpaper & style" and after accessing the Emoji Workshop, first change the background.
   - Select Edit Emoji from the menu that appears on the right side of the screen. Proceed by tapping Done.
   - Pick out an emoji.

     Regarding a certain emoji: Pick up the keyboard. Up to fourteen different emojis are at your disposal for use as wallpaper.

     For a haphazard collection: Select the "Randomize" option.

2. Decide on a design and measurement:
   - Choose Patterns from the panel at the bottom.
   - Make your pattern choice.
   - Make use of the slider to alter the size of the pattern's emojis.

3. Pick out a hue:
   - Locate the Colors panel and press on it.
   - Color your wallpaper.
4. View the wallpaper options and choose one:
   - Select Home screen from the Lock screen menu to get a preview of your emoji wallpaper.
   - Tap Set wallpaper after you're satisfied with the preview.
   - The Home screen or the Home and lock screens allow you to choose the position of your wallpaper.

Make AI-powered backgrounds for the Pixel 8 and Pixel 8 Pro

Some account types, such as Family Link accounts, may not have access to AI wallpapers.

Using your instructions, generative AI can make wallpapers that are unique to you. Here are some options:

- Use the existing wallpaper settings to access the new wallpaper.
- An example prompt is provided; all you have to do is fill it out.

- Adjust the end product to your liking by selecting various settings.
- Keep your wallpapers for future use.

The process to create artificial intelligence wallpaper is:

1. Find an empty spot on your phone's home screen then press and hold.
2. To access more wallpapers, go to Wallpaper & style, then tap on AI wallpaper.
3. To make your artificial intelligence wallpaper, choose a topic.
4. Select a random question and then tap "Inspire me" to get a matching wallpaper.
5. To access certain choices, tap the highlighted word in the question.
6. Make wallpaper by tapping the Create wallpaper button.
7. Swipe left or right to choose from a variety of backgrounds created by artificial intelligence.
8. Pick either the Home screen or the Lock screen, then press Done to set the wallpaper.

The wallpaper is kept after each usage, so you may use it again and again.

Personalize your Pixel Fold's clock face

1. Locate an empty area on your phone's home screen by touching and holding it.
2. Select the Lock screen from the Wallpaper & style menu.
3. Press and hold the "Clock color & size" caption to see the style choices.
4. Choose a color by tapping on Color.
5. Use the slider to adjust the brightness and contrast of the color.
   - Choose the desired size by tapping the Size button.
   - The size of the clock dynamically varies based on the content on the lock screen.
6. Press the left arrow to apply your style changes.

Modify the appearance of the home screen (Pixel 2 and later)

Fonts, icon shapes, and color schemes for the Home screen may be customized by:

1. Find an empty spot on your phone's home screen then press and hold.
2. Select Wallpaper and style.
3. Select between the Basic colors or Wallpaper colors.
4. Make a selection.
5. Press either Apply or Done.

(Pixel 3 and later) Modify the grid layout of the home screen

On the Home screen, you may adjust the grid size by:

1. Find an empty spot on your phone's home screen then press and hold.
2. Select Wallpaper and style.
3. Tap the App grid at the bottom.
4. Please choose a grid size.
5. Press Finish.

For Pixel 4 and before, set new wallpaper every day.

1. Locate an empty area on your phone's home screen by touching and holding it.
2. Select Wallpaper and style.
3. Press on Reset Wallpaper.
   - You can't use your photographs or live wallpapers with daily wallpaper.
4. Click on a category of wallpapers.
5. Press on "Daily wallpaper" in the upper right corner.
6. Select Okay.

Make use of icons that fit a certain theme.

Adapt the icons of compatible apps to the color palette of your phone:

1. Find an empty spot on your phone's home screen then press and hold.
2. Select Wallpaper and style.
3. You may toggle it on and off by tapping the themed icons at the bottom.

ORGANIZE YOUR HOME SCREENS WITH WIDGETS

Organize your home screens with widgets, shortcuts, and applications.

You may personalize your home screens to easily access the information you love. A user may arrange and include:

- Apps
- Quick links to within-app content
- Info widgets that don't need launching applications

Android 9.0 and later are required to complete some of these tasks.

INCLUDE ON HOME SCREENS

Include a mobile app

1. Pull up the Home screen by swiping up from the bottom.
2. Move the app using your finger. Pictured below are all of the Home screens.
3. Move the app to the spot you like. Gesture upwards.

Include a shortcut

1. Raise your finger while touching and holding the app. Shortcuts will be shown if they are available in the app.
2. To use the shortcut, touch and hold it.
3. You may move the shortcut to any location you like. Gesture upwards.

Tapping a shortcut allows you to utilize it without adding it to the Home screen.

Toggle the size of a widget

Combine widgets

1. Press and hold an empty area on the Home screen.
2. Select Widgets.

3. Look for a program that offers the widget you want.
4. By tapping the app, you can see the list of widgets that are compatible with it.
5. Locate and grasp a widget. Pictures of your Home screens will be sent to you.
6. Move the widget to the desired location. Gesture upwards.

You may find widgets in certain applications. The app may be tapped and held. Press Widgets thereafter.

Widget resizing

1. Grab the widget from your Home screen with a touch.
2. Gesture upwards. There will be dots on the sides of the widget's outline if it can be enlarged.
3. Simply drag the dots to adjust the widget's size.
4. Tap outside the widget after you're done.

GET YOUR HOME SCREENS IN ORDER
Arrange files into a folder

1. A shortcut or program may be touched and held.
2. Place that shortcut or program on top of another by dragging it. Gesture upwards.

- To add more, just drag and drop each item into the group.
- Select the group by tapping on it. Choose the recommended folder and then touch on it. You may also choose a name from the list that appears at the top of the keyboard or enter your own.

Shift a widget, app, shortcut, or group

1. Navigate by touching and dragging the object. Pictures of your Home screens will be sent to you.
2. Simply drag the object to the desired location.
3. Gesture upwards.

The "At A Glance" information located at the top of your Pixel phone's screen cannot be moved.

Take out a program, shortcut, widget, or set of them.

1. Get your hands on it and feel it.
2. Press and hold the object until you see the "Remove" button.
3. Gesture upwards.

"Remove," "Uninstall," or even both may be available to you. Just removing an app from your

Home screen is what "Remove" does. Choose "Uninstall" to remove it from your device.

The "At A Glance" information located at the top of your Pixel phone's screen cannot be moved.

Establish a Start menu

1. Press and hold an app, shortcut, or collection.
2. To access the Home screen without any content, slide it to the right.
3. Gesture upwards.

Take a home screen off

1. Clear the Home screen of any shortcuts, applications, widgets, or groups you no longer need.
2. When all of them are gone, the Home screen will follow suit.

CREATE A PERSONALIZED HOME SCREEN
Update details at the very top

"At A Glance" information is located at the top of your primary Home screen. As an example, you may get information regarding:

- The date
- Every day's forecast
- Who or what do you have scheduled next?

- Reminds you when your Nest package is due
- Airlines' luggage claim details

Changing the shown information:

1. Locate the area and press down on it.
2. Select Settings from the Customize menu.

Swap out a program

A row of your most-used applications may be seen at the very bottom of your screen.

- Get rid of a beloved app: To delete an app from your favorites, tap and hold it. Reposition it on the screen by dragging it.
- Include a beloved app: Then, swipe up from the bottom of the screen. Locate and tap an app. Place the app in a vacant location next to your favorites.

Alter more options on the Home screen

1. Press and hold an empty area on the Home screen.
2. Select the "Home" option.

Activate or deactivate the search bar animations.

The search bar on the Home screen may sometimes display animations. On occasion, like holidays, the animations will be available for a limited time.

You may disable or enable these animations by touching and holding the search bar.

1. Go to Preferences by tapping More.
2. Make the search box effects active or inactive.

SWAP OUT YOUR GO-TO APPLICATIONS

You can see a list of all your installed applications at the bottom of the screen. Your phone will recommend applications to your favorites depending on your habits, the apps you've recently used, and the apps you use the most. A colorful shadow encircles the icon of the app you recommended.

The row will refresh with a new recommended app whenever there is a blank spot. Any of the recommended applications may be pinned, removed, or added. Another option is to replace an app by hand.

Secure a mobile app

1. Press and hold the app that was recommended.
2. Click on Pin in the top right corner of the menu.

Get rid of a beloved app

1. Press and hold the app that was recommended.
2. Click on Pin in the top right corner of the menu.

You can prevent an app from being suggested by touching and dragging it to the "Don't suggest app" option.

Disable in-app recommendations for the apps you love.

Recommendations will not be available once you disable them until you re-enable them.

1. Locate an empty area on your phone's home screen by touching and holding it.
2. Select Home > Settings > Suggestions.
3. Pick whether to activate:
   - All applications' suggestions display recommendations on the main screen

Incorporate a valued app

To manually add an app to your favorites list, you must first disable app recommendations in the Home screen settings.

1. Then, swipe up from the bottom of the screen.
2. Locate and tap an app.

3. Transfer the app to a vacant location next to your preferred apps.
4. Gesture upwards.

TAKE CHARGE OF YOUR SCREEN AND DISPLAY OPTIONS

Several options are available, including the ability to adjust the screen's brightness, text size, display size, and rotation.

- Android 10 and later are required to complete some of these procedures.
- Touching the screen is necessary for some of these procedures.

MODIFY THE DISPLAY PARAMETERS

1. Go to the Settings app on your phone.
2. Touch the screen.
3. Select the option you want to modify by tapping on it. To access further options, choose Advanced.

Quick options allow you to access your most often-used options from any screen.

ADJUST THE DISPLAY OPTIONS

Light intensity controls

- Slide the Brightness level slider to adjust the brightness of your screen.
- Adjustable light intensity
By using Adaptive brightness, your screen's brightness will be adjusted automatically to match the ambient light. The default setting has this turned on. Adaptive brightness allows you to adjust the brightness of your screen. Your phone will eventually figure out what you like.

Adaptive brightness on Pixel 4 and subsequent Pixel phones may momentarily increase the screen's brightness above its typical maximum, making it easier to read in exceptionally strong ambient illumination, like as direct sunshine.

- Sombre design

Navigate to the Dark theme. Reduce power consumption by making the backdrop of various displays on your phone darker. You have the option to program the Dark theme to activate at certain intervals.

- Light at Night

You have the power to make your phone more readable in low light.

Configuration of the screen

- Styles and backgrounds for Pixel 2 and later: Alter the background image, typography, icon shape, and accent color of your phone.
- Background image (Pixel 1 only): Use your photographs, the live wallpapers, or the defaults as your background.
- Icons with a certain theme

  To make the compatible app icons fit your phone's color scheme, you may change them.

- Sombre design

  A dark color scheme might help you preserve battery life on some panels, such as the Settings app. Navigate to the Dark theme.

- Pause the screen

  Determine the time it takes for your phone's screen to turn off while it's not in use.

- (Pixel 4 and after) focus on screen

  No matter how long you stare at it, you should always have the screen on.

- Screen attention is most effective in a well-lit environment, away from direct sunshine.

- Ask Google Assistant, "How can I extend the time that my phone remains unlocked?" on your Pixel 8 or Pixel 8 Pro.
- External Equalizer (Pixel 4 only)

  Adapt the color temperature of your screen to the ambient light automatically.

- Display with Little Bump

  The refresh rate may be automatically increased for certain types of content: Advice: Doing so raises the battery load.

- Pixel 7 and 7a - as high as 90 Hz
- Pixel 7 Pro - 120 Hz onwards
- A desktop background

  You may use a screen saver to display images, vibrant backdrops, and more while your phone charges.

- Display on the lock screen
- Protected area: You get to decide how your lock screen displays alerts.
- Message that appears on locked screens Put some text on your lock screen.
- Enable the lockdown feature.

- Duplex line timer: You may customize the lock screen clock to show either two lines or one line.
- Right now While playing, you may easily recognize nearby music.
- Pixel 4 only: Idle lock screen Set your phone to wake up when you're close by, or leave it on all the time.
- Except for the Pixel 4, all Pixel phones always display the time and information: Keep an eye on the time and a few other metrics even when you turn off your display.
- Press to view phone: By tapping your screen twice, you may access certain information.
- Rise to examine the phone: Upon picking up your phone, check your alerts.
- Upcoming announcements: Keep an eye on the lock screen for any fresh alerts.
- Primary hues
- Realistic: View colors as they appear.
- Improved: View truer colors with more vibrancy. For Pixel 2, this is turned on by default.
- Adaptive (Pixel 3 and later): Enjoy the full range of colors while preserving their finer nuances. It is enabled automatically.
- Congested (Pixel 2 exclusively): Experience the most vibrant hues.

Adjustments for visibility

- Size of the font
- Size the text on your screen to your liking.
- Size of display
- You may resize the objects on your screen.
- Screen rotation on demand
- Rotate the content that appears on your phone's screen as you spin it.

  You can still rotate the screen even when Auto-rotation is off. Turn your phone around, and then hit the Rotate button in the corner.

- As soon as the phone enters virtual reality mode

  In virtual reality mode, you may adjust your phone to minimize blur or flicker.

USE YOUR PIXEL PHONE TO CALL FOR AID

In case of an emergency, use your Pixel phone to call for aid.

Put your emergency contact information in the Personal Safety app and share it with others. In certain countries and with some carriers, your phone can automatically contact emergency services.

Android 13 and later are required to complete some of these tasks.

MAKE CONTINGENCY PLANS

Even when you lock your phone, anybody who gets their hands on it may see your lock screen message and emergency details. This feature may be disabled in the Personal Safety app.

Consult the Personal Safety app.

Every Pixel phone comes with the Personal Safety app. Fold and all Pixel 4a and later devices automatically download the app.

To deactivate the Personal Safety app so it doesn't appear on your app list.

On a Pixel 3a or before, install the Personal Safety app.

1. Make sure you're running the most recent version of Android.
2. After you go to Settings, choose about phone.
3. Press the button for important details.
4. Select Update from the banner located at the top of the screen.

Your options

- Even without installing the app, on Pixel 3a and older: Use your Google Account to log in, then add people to your emergency contact list and medical history.
- Upon installation of the app: Some of the features include a safety check, crisis notifications, sharing in an emergency, and the ability to detect car crashes. Pixel 4a and subsequent models, including the Fold, come with car collision detection.

Things required

Turning on Location Services and granting permissions are necessary for the Personal Safety app to function. Depending on the user type, you may not be able to utilize Location Sharing in all countries.

With Location Sharing, you may let others know where you are in the world right now from your mobile devices. All of your Google products, including Maps, will display your name, picture, and current location when you share them with someone. Here is some information about your shared location:

- Particular places you have been or are now located.

- Your present pursuits, such as walking or driving.
- Details about your gadget, such as its battery life or GPS connectivity.
- For example, "started a call" or "called local emergency number" may be your call status.
- Where you are, such as your house, place of employment, or vacation spot.

Enhance the Personal Safety app with crucial emergency details

Information like as your blood type, allergies, and prescriptions may be added to the lock screen of your phone in case of an emergency.

1. Launch the Safeguard app on your mobile device.
2. Enter your Google Account credentials when prompted.
3. Get in touch with your details.
4. Include your contact information in case of an emergency.
   - Regarding Health Documents:
   - Press on Health records.
   - Press the item you want to edit in the list to provide new information, such as a prescription or allergy history.
   - In the event of an emergency:

- Hit the "Emergency contacts" button and then Create a contact and after that, You want to include an existing contact.
- Press the Allow access to emergency data and Show when locked buttons to display your emergency information even when the screen is locked.
- Get your phone ready to use a SIM card or an eSIM. You won't be able to subsequently text your emergency contact if this doesn't happen.

Auto-Crash Detection Mode On

Upon detecting a serious vehicle accident, your phone can instantly contact emergency services, such as 911 in the United States, and provide your precise position.

For the car collision detection feature to function, your phone must have a SIM card.

1. Launch the Safeguard app on your mobile device.
2. Press on Features.
3. Down the page, you should see "Car crash detection."
4. Go to the Set up menu.
   - While the app is open, hit Allow when prompted to disclose your location.

- Select Allow when prompted to share your microphone and activities.

METHODS FOR IDENTIFYING VEHICLE CRASH

Information including your phone's position, motion sensors, and adjacent noises may be used by Pixel 4a and subsequent phones, including Fold, to predict a probable serious vehicle accident. To function, vehicle collision detection systems need access to the user's location, level of physical activity, and microphone. Your phone can notify emergency services in the event of an automobile collision. You could be asked to provide your location and what transpired during this conversation, since it makes use of Android's Emergency Location Service.

Some crashes could go unnoticed by your phone. Car collision detection might potentially be triggered by high-impact activities. Your Pixel phone may have trouble contacting emergency services in some situations. The strength of your mobile network may be low, or you may be in the middle of a lengthy conversation.

When and when road collision detection is accessible

Car collision detection is supported in the following languages on Pixel 4a and later, which includes Fold:

- Danish native
- Dutch
- Various languages
- Canadian French
- Japanese, Mandarin Chinese, Italian
- Spanish, Norwegian, and Swedish

Regarding the areas or nations listed below:

- The nation of Australia
- Belgium Italy Austria
- North America
- The Danish
- The French
- India
- Japan, Ireland, and Italy
- Netherlands, Norway
- Portugal
- Malaysia Singapore
- The Spanish
- The Nordic nation

- The Swiss
- United Kingdom, Taiwan,
- US

Install and disable Emergency SOS

Using your phone in an emergency allows you to do things like call for assistance, share your position with those you've designated as an emergency contact, and even capture video.

- For the car collision detection feature to function, your phone needs a SIM card.
- Neither airplane mode nor Battery Saver will activate Emergency SOS.
- All Pixel 4a and subsequent models, including Fold, come with Emergency SOS.

Configure and activate Emergency SOS

1. Go to the Settings app on your phone.
2. Press the Safety and emergency button, followed by Emergency SOS.
3. Tap on "Start setup" located at the bottom.
4. My phone has an emergency button that I may press in case I need assistance.
   - Press the Start button to enter your emergency contact information.

- Select "Change number" if you'd like to update the local emergency contact information.
- After you have the right local number, hit the Next button.
- To let emergency personnel know where you are if you are unable to speak, you may enable assisted calling on your phone.
- Select "Turn on" to enable assisted calling.
- The availability of assisted calling is locale-dependent.
- By selecting Start setup and then Set up, you may share your position with emergency contacts and give them updates.
- Select a person to whom you would want to send emergency information by tapping the Add contact button.
- Pick the details you want your emergency contact to have access to from Emergency SOS.
- Press the "Next" button.
- Allowing the Personal Safety app to access your location while using the app is necessary to communicate your location in the event of an emergency.
- Continue by clicking the Next button, and after that During the whole app experience.

- If you need an emergency SOS You may begin making an emergency audio recording without interrupting your current activity by scrolling down and tapping the "Start setup" button.
- Select Turn on and then begin recording emergency footage. During the whole app experience.
- You have the option to automatically share your video with your emergency contacts after it's stored on your smartphone. Click Next after selecting Share automatically after backup.
- Select one of the following to initiate the Emergency SOS procedures:
- Press and hold to initiate activities.
- After the countdown finishes, click on Start activities. Select "Play alarm sound" to activate the feature's alarm function.

5. Hit the Finish button.

Select an option to launch Emergency SOS

You have the option to configure Emergency SOS to initiate the emergency actions automatically or to prompt a confirmation step before their commencement.

1. Go to the Settings app on your phone.

2. Select Safety & emergency, and then push the SOS button.
3. Next to "How it works," choose "Settings."
4. There are two methods to configure Emergency SOS:
   - Press and hold to initiate an emergency action to include a confirmation step.
   - Press Start activities automatically after the 5-second countdown to initiate automatic emergency actions.

Exit the Emergency SOS mode

1. Go to the Settings app on your phone.
2. Select Safety & emergency, and then push the SOS button.
3. Next to "How it works," choose "Settings."
4. Tap Exit the Emergency SOS mode.

Personalize your lock screen with a message

1. Go to the Settings app on your phone.
2. Select "Display" followed by "Lock screen." Following that, Insert text onto the lock screen.
3. Please enter your message, including any details that might be used to recover your missing phone.
4. Hit the Save button.

Manage the broadcasting of critical alerts

This is where you may adjust the settings for certain types of emergency messages, such as those that warn of impending danger, specific threats, or AMBER alerts.

Notification kinds may be toggled on and off, alert history can be accessed, and vibration and volume can be adjusted.

1. Launch the Settings app on your mobile device.
2. Select Wireless emergency alerts from the Notifications menu.
3. Select the options you want to enable and the frequency with which you would like to receive notifications.

CALL FOR ASSISTANCE IN A TIME OF CRISIS

(Pixel 3 and subsequent models, including Pixel Fold) Obtain assistance in the event of an impact

When the battery saver is on or you are in Airplane mode, the car accident detection feature will not function. When you're on the go, auto collision detection won't operate; it's country-specific.

Your phone may identify whether you were in a serious automobile collision when you switched on car crash detection. Not only will your phone vibrate and make an alert, but it will also ask you out loud and on the screen whether you need assistance.

Within sixty seconds, you will be given the option to either terminate the call or contact emergency services.

Get in touch with the authorities in case of an emergency.

- Say "Emergency" or move the slider to Call 911 and inform contacts if Emergency Sharing is enabled.
- By default, your phone will go to speakerphone mode.

Get out of here!

- Select "Cancel" or press the "I'm OK" button.
- You can't make an urgent call on your phone.

Within sixty seconds, if you haven't replied

- Without your intervention, your phone will go into loudspeaker mode, attempt to contact emergency services, falsely report an automobile accident, and divulge your device's precise whereabouts.

- Though it will play again, you have the option to talk over it. Press Cancel to end the message and continue the call.

Get in touch with loved ones, send a distress signal, and capture footage using Emergency SOS.

Turning on Battery Saver or flying into an aircraft will disable Emergency SOS.

Using your phone in an emergency allows you to do things like call for assistance, share your position with those you've designated as an emergency contact, and even capture video.

1. Hold down the power button on your phone for at least five seconds.
2. To initiate the emergency call, either tap and hold the red circle for three seconds or wait for the countdown to begin automatically, depending on your settings.
3. Depending on your settings, further emergency activities will commence when you initiate an emergency call.

Enable Emergency Sharing and video recording before placing your call to emergency services. These features will begin recording automatically.

UNINTENTIONAL PHONE CONVERSATIONS

Do not end the call if you accidentally dial 911. It was an accident, therefore you don't need help; just tell the emergency operator that.

Capture footage during a crisis

Important: The purpose of video recording is to help you stay safe by allowing you to capture important moments and associated occurrences. We may record your usage of the app, sharing with emergency contacts, and video link views/downloads when you use our products to record, upload, and share audio and video material, such as recordings of an emergency. This logging is in addition to what is stated in our Privacy Policy. Your emergency contacts may experience distress if they are disturbed by recordings of emergency incidents. Take caution while using the video-sharing function. If you want to use this tool, you need to make sure you follow all the rules, including federal and state laws against wiretapping and video recording. You agree and recognize the above by using this function.

The process of emergency recording

Even with emergency recording turned on, your phone may still serve other purposes, such as alerting loved ones of your whereabouts or contacting nearby emergency services.

The emergency recording will stop if you launch another app that utilizes your camera. A gray screen will appear on your recording when emergency recording is halted. Reopen the Personal Safety app or press the alert in the upper right corner of the screen to return to your emergency recording.

Up to 45 minutes of video may be recorded and saved in an emergency. About 10 megabytes per minute is the quality of the video.

The process of auto-sharing

With auto share enabled, every time you shoot a video, a link to it will be sent to all of your emergency contacts automatically. Your footage won't be shared with anybody unless you set up Emergency Contacts. You will have fifteen seconds after recording to discontinue sharing the video if you change your mind. It all comes down to your internet connection speed when it comes to how long it takes to upload and distribute your finished film. You may make sure that anybody who wants to see your video in an emergency can download it.

At any given moment, a video may only have one active sharing link. The purpose of the 7-day expiry limit is to safeguard your privacy when you establish a connection. Any time you choose, you may turn off a connection. Turn off the old connection and make a new one to reset the expiry timer. For a sharing link to be disabled:

1. Tap on the Personal Safety app on your phone.
2. Go to Your details, and then tap on Your videos.
3. Select More, then Delete, and finally Delete, next to a video.

If you want to stay safe in an emergency, you should utilize an emergency recording. Excessive sharing of an active shared link will cause Google to deactivate it automatically. If the unique sharing link is visited more than 120 times, it is considered excessive sharing.

Functions of automatic backup

Records in case of an emergency are immediately uploaded to the cloud. Your data will be better protected if your phone is lost or damaged in an emergency if you do. If you're on a metered network, uploading to the cloud can eat up your data plan. Any time you have an online connection, you may manage your uploaded emergency recordings. For video management:

1. Tap on the Personal Safety app on your phone.
2. Go to Your details, and then tap on Your videos.
3. Press More next to a video, and then choose Share or Delete.

There is no way to restore a file you've erased from your Google Account.

Locate critical details

1. You may unlock a screen by swiping it up.
2. Hit the "Emergency" button and then Check out the safety data.

Automate the transmission of your position

When you call or text an emergency number, such as 911 in the US or 112 in Europe, your phone's location may be communicated. This helps rescuers locate you faster.

If you haven't disabled Android's emergency location service (ELS), and the feature is available in your nation or area and on your mobile network, your phone will automatically notify first responders of its whereabouts. Your cell provider may still transmit the device's position in the event of an emergency even if ELS is off.

Manage the status of the Emergency Location Service.

1. Launch the Settings app on your mobile device.
2. Select Emergency Location Service or Google Emergency Location Service from the list of services under Location.
3. You may toggle the use of Emergency Location Service and Google, respectively, on and off.

Systematic Approach to Emergency Location Service

Only when you dial or text an emergency number does your phone utilize Emergency Location Service (ELS).

If your phone's emergency location services (ELS) are enabled, it will utilize information such as Google Location Services to pinpoint your exact position in the event of an emergency. In addition, ELS could transmit further data, such as the language your device is configured with.

Your phone shares this information with approved emergency response agencies so they can find you and aid you. This information does not go via Google but rather straight from your phone to emergency services.

Google receives use, statistics, and diagnostics data from your phone once an ELS-enabled call or text is complete via Google Play Services. Google will just use this information to evaluate ELS; they will not acquire any personal details, such as your location, in this process.

Unlike sharing your position with Google Maps, the procedure of sending your location with ELS is distinct.

Make sure your emergency contacts know where you are at all times.

Your emergency contacts will be able to see your current position and get notifications about your battery life. The Personal Safety app can't access your whereabouts without your explicit consent.

Emergency sharing may only be used if you have:

• Remember to have the number of an emergency contact handy.

- Tap the "While in Use" button to provide the Personal Safety app access to your location.
- A notice will show up in the Personal Safety app if Location Sharing is not accessible in your country. This is significant.
- Make sure you're connected to the internet and have Location Services enabled.
- Start sharing the status of emergency calls.

Gets the ball rolling on emergency sharing

1. Tap on the Personal Safety app on your phone.
2. Select the option for sharing in an emergency.
3. Pick the people you want to share your current whereabouts with in real-time.
   - Include a note if you'd like.
4. Select Share.
5. To see the specifics of your emergency sharing, tap the banner that appears in the message.

Immediately cease distributing emergency information.

1. Tap on the Personal Safety app on your phone.
2. Press the information sharing emergency button.
3. Select Stop.
   - Feel free to provide a letter that clarifies the reason for terminating the emergency sharing.

The automatic termination of emergency sharing occurs after twenty-four hours.

Sharing emergency information when detecting car crashes

You may configure your phone to initiate Emergency Sharing in the case of a collision if you have Car crash detection enabled.

Disable auto-crash alerts and enable emergency sharing

1. Tap on the Personal Safety app on your phone.
2. Press on Features at the very bottom.
3. Hit the "Car crash detection" button.
4. For immediate action in the event of an accident, activate your phone's emergency mode.
   - Choose Emergency Sharing to notify those you've designated as contacts in case of an emergency of your current whereabouts and any changes.

The vehicle will immediately contact emergency services if the accident detection feature is activated.

- Within 60 seconds of a crash being identified, you will have the option to terminate the call by tapping the "I'm OK" button.

- Get in touch with loved ones by using the "Call 911" button.

Just say "Hey Google, start Emergency Sharing" to have Google Assistant begin sharing your location in an emergency.

You may set up a Safety Check or notify emergency contacts of your whereabouts simply by speaking to Google Assistant. Distinctions from the Personal Safety app include:

- Safety Check with Assistant isn't going to notify your emergency contacts by text message when you start Personal Safety.
- Choosing a contact from your contact list is not an option while using Emergency Sharing with Assistant. You may notify everyone on your emergency contact list with the help of Emergency Sharing.

Just ask Google Assistant to begin or end a safety check:

- "Go ahead, Google! Launch a Safety Check."
- For the length of [time], "Hey Google, begin a Safety Check."

The duration of your safety check might range from one minute to twenty-four hours.

- Google, disable Safety Check, please.

Just ask Google Assistant to begin or stop emergency sharing:

- "Allow Emergency Sharing to begin, Google."
- "Calm down, Google. Emergency Sharing is over."

Set up a preventative inspection

You may set up a safety check so that your phone will monitor your whereabouts and notify your emergency contacts in the event of an emergency. When venturing out into a new region or attending a social event, for instance, it's wise to do a safety check. Permitting the Personal Safety app to use your location when it's "While in Use" is a necessity.

1. Tap on the Personal Safety app on your phone.
2. Select the "Safety check" option.
3. Please provide the Reason and Duration. A time interval of 15 minutes to 8 hours may be specified for the check.
4. Next, choose Next.
5. Choose your phone number(s).
6. Press the Start button.

If you have your emergency contacts set up to receive texts, they will get a message with:

- The name you want.
- What time your safety check will take?
- Justify your position, if you so desire.

TAKE PRECAUTIONS BY MARKING YOURSELF SAFE

You will get a 60-second warning before emergency sharing starts when it is time to check-in. You may terminate the emergency sharing by marking yourself as safe. At any moment, you may disable Safety Check by simply receiving a message. Emergency sharing will start if you don't choose an option within 60 seconds.

1. Select an option from the list that appears when you get the notification:
   - I'm okay. Stay Private.
   - Jump right in and start taking part. There will be no further safety inspections after this.
   - Make an emergency 911 call.
2. Unlocking your phone can be necessary if it is locked.

No matter what happens to your phone, Safety Check will keep running. At the appointed check-in time, the precaution will begin disclosing your last known location in the event of an emergency.

Methods for notifying people in case of urgency

Notifications sent to emergency contacts by Google when emergency sharing is activated include:

- The person whose name it is
- One way to get Google Maps in real-time
- The amount of battery life you have left
- A note, should you have supplied one

Marking oneself safe or manually stopping emergency sharing and safety checks are other options. As soon as they cease, Google will notify your contacts by text message that your Safety check is over.

Obtain notifications in the event of an emergency

In a national or local emergency, such as a natural catastrophe, the Personal Safety app will notify you if you have enabled crisis notifications. A link to the site of the Personal Safety app is included in crisis alert alerts so that you may access more information about the event.

Any country or language may get a crisis notice. If your phone's language settings are not in sync with the local language, the notice can be shown in the official language of your present location rather than your default language.

ENABLE OR DISABLE CRISIS NOTIFICATIONS

1. Launch the Safeguard app on your mobile device.
2. To get crisis notifications, tap on Features.
3. Enable or disable crisis notifications.

What Google does when a catastrophe occurs

Crisis information is handled by Google using approved local sources. The Personal Safety app will alert you if a situation is reported that impacts your current location. The effect on the ground, official information from governments and other agencies, and internet connection in the impacted region are some of the elements that Google considers when posting crisis warnings. Usually, you may get an alert in English and the main language of the impacted region.

Reach out to emergency services with the help of Fast Emergency Dialer.

Even if your phone is locked, you may still use it to swiftly summon emergency services.

Get a backup phone system set up

107

The Personal Safety app allows you to contact emergency services:

- You may swiftly summon assistance with a slider swipe using the Fast Emergency Dialer (FED). The local emergency numbers are automatically displayed.
- If you need to call an emergency number quickly, you may see a dialpad on the Traditional Emergency Dialer (TED).

When FED is available, Pixel phones are configured to utilize it automatically.

Rapid Dialer for Emergencies

- Easy access: Make a single call to an emergency number by sliding the slider.
- Numbers for automatic emergencies: No matter where you are, your phone will always be able to locate emergency numbers.
- Numerous emergency contact numbers: For local emergency services like police, fire, and medical, your phone can look up accessible numbers. To choose the appropriate emergency service, just use the slider.

Quick Emergency Dialer: A User's Guide

On devices running Android 11 or earlier, or Pixel 5 or earlier running Android 12:

1. Maintain a 5-second hold on the power button.
2. Press the emergency button.
3. Utilize the slider located in the emergency menu.

On devices running Android 12 or later, as well as Pixel 6 and later, you may access the following controls:

1. To turn the volume up and power on simultaneously, press and hold both buttons.
2. Press the emergency button.
3. Utilize the slider located in the emergency menu.

Availability of a Quick Emergency Dialer

Not all locations or locales provide FED. Even in covered locations, FED and its availability might be limited by your carrier and other factors.

If FED is unavailable, your phone will switch to TED, which will show you a dial pad that you may use to summon emergency services. Your emergency dialer settings remain the same when FED is unavailable.

SEND OUT 911 CALLS WITH ASSISTANCE

An "Emergency Number" screen with information and tools to assist during an emergency will appear on a Pixel phone when you call an emergency number, such as 911 in the US.

- You may go back to a regular voice call if necessary; these capabilities should be familiar to most emergency operators.
- Requires no connectivity to the internet
- Quick and easy setup

Determine where you are in the event of a crisis

To help the emergency operator find you, you may show them your current position on your screen. What your phone can detect might determine what you find:

- Complete street address
- Added code (such as "CWC8+JH")
- The coordinates of a location may be expressed simply using plus codes.
- They are identifiable to emergency personnel.
- Using coordinates such as "37.4216105,-122.0857449" for longitude and latitude
- Road map

Subtly notify a supervisor (choose sites)

This function is currently only accessible in the following countries: Australia, Canada, Denmark, France, Ireland, Italy, Japan, Norway, Singapore, Spain, Sweden, Taiwan, the United Kingdom, and the United States.

Select "Medical," "Fire," or "Police" to silently notify an emergency operator.

You won't hear a thing on your phone. However, the emergency operator will detect:

- The fact that this is a voice-activated bot
- The assistance you need
- (We only accept orders from the US, UK, and Australia)
- If it is provided via your device's built-in Emergency Information or another source, your name

Learn more about local earthquake hazards

When an earthquake occurs nearby, your phone may notify you. Get more information on earthquakes in your area by opening Google Search and entering "earthquake in [your city or region]."

Just off Google Location Accuracy on your phone if you don't want it to help in earthquake detection.

Learn about impending earthquakes in your area

Pacific Northwest states

If there is an earthquake in the area with a magnitude of 4.5 or higher, your phone may utilize your approximate position to notify you. Data from ShakeAlert is used to generate these earthquake notifications.

Oceania and the Greek Isles

If there is an earthquake in the area with a magnitude of 4.5 or higher, your phone may utilize your approximate position to notify you. An Android Earthquake Alerts System is the foundation of these seismic warnings.

Enable or disable earthquake notifications.

Make sure you have Wi-Fi or data enabled if you want to get notifications.

1. Go to the Settings app on your phone.

2. Select "Safety & Escrow" Earthquake warnings follow.
3. Change the status of Earthquake notifications.

By design, earthquake warnings are enabled. Not all earthquakes in your region will trigger an alert, and you will only be notified in countries that are compatible with our system. On rare occasions, an earthquake may be detected but not felt where you are.

CHAPTER FOUR

WALLPAPERS MAY BE MADE OR CUSTOMIZED

Wallpapers may be made or customized with Pixel 6 and subsequent versions, including Fold.

Wallpaper brightness is reduced when power saving is on.

You may express your individuality and make it uniquely yours using the new Pixel phone features. Make your one-of-a-kind wallpapers by enhancing your photographs with 3D effects and motion graphics. With Emoji Workshop, you can even make your wallpapers.

For Pixel 6 and later, including Fold, you may apply effects to your picture wallpapers.

1. Locate an empty area on your phone's home screen by touching and holding it.
2. Press on Wallpaper, and then choose My pictures.
3. Pick a picture.
4. Click on Effects.
5. To make a cinematic wallpaper, turn it on.

6. Select the Lock screen from the Home screen to preview your wallpaper.
7. Use the Home screen, Lock screen, or both screens to choose where to set your wallpaper.

For Pixel 4a and later, including Fold, you may use Emoji Workshop to make your wallpapers.

You have the freedom to personalize your wallpapers using emojis, patterns, and background colors. These personalized emoji backgrounds are downloadable.

PICK OUT AN EMOJI

Choose from a variety of emoji or choose one you like.

1. Locate an empty area on your phone's home screen by touching and holding it.
2. To access the Emoji Workshop, first, tap on Wallpaper & style, then choose Change wallpaper.
3. Select Edit Emoji from the menu that appears on the right side of the screen. Proceed by tapping Done.
4. Pick out an emoji.
   - Regarding a certain emoji: Pick up the keyboard. Up to fourteen different emojis are at your disposal for use as wallpaper.

- For a haphazard collection: Select the "Randomize" option.

DECIDE ON A STYLE AND SIZE

You may change the pattern of your emojis when you pick a background.

1. Choose Patterns from the panel at the bottom.
2. Make your pattern choice.
3. Make use of the slider to alter the size of the pattern's emojis.

CHOOSE A SHADE

1. Locate the Colors panel and press on it.
2. Color your wallpaper.

SEE THE WALLPAPER & CHOOSE IT

1. Select Home screen from the Lock screen menu to get a preview of your emoji wallpaper.
2. Tap Set wallpaper after you're satisfied with the preview.
3. The Home screen or the Home and lock screens allow you to choose the position of your wallpaper.

Make AI-powered backgrounds for the Pixel 8 and Pixel 8 Pro

Some account types, such as Family Link accounts, may not have access to AI wallpapers.

Using your instructions, generative AI can make wallpapers that are unique to you. I can help you out:

- Use the existing wallpaper settings to access the new wallpaper.
- An example prompt is provided; all you have to do is fill it out.
- Adjust the end product to your liking by selecting various settings.
- Keep your wallpapers for future use.

The process to create artificial intelligence wallpaper is:

1. Find an empty spot on your phone's home screen then press and hold.
2. To access more wallpapers, go to Wallpaper & style, then tap on AI wallpaper.
3. To make your artificial intelligence wallpaper, choose a topic.
4. Select a random question and then tap "Inspire me" to get a matching wallpaper.
5. To access certain choices, tap the highlighted word in the question.
6. Make wallpaper by tapping the Create wallpaper button.

7. Swipe left or right to choose from a variety of backgrounds created by artificial intelligence.
8. Pick either the Home screen or the Lock screen, then press Done to set the wallpaper.

The wallpaper is kept after each usage, so you may use it again and again.

Personalize your Pixel Fold's clock face

1. Locate an empty area on your phone's home screen by touching and holding it.
2. Select the Lock screen from the Wallpaper & style menu.
3. Press and hold the "Clock color & size" caption to see the style choices.
4. Choose a color by tapping on Color.
   - Use the slider to adjust the brightness and contrast of the color.
5. Choose the desired size by tapping the Size button.
   - The size of the clock dynamically varies based on the content on the lock screen.
   - Press the left arrow to apply your style changes.

USE YOUR PIXEL PHONE AS A NAVIGATOR

Some of these instructions are only compatible with Android 11 and later. Locate the Android version checker and familiarize yourself with its steps.

PICK A MODE OF TRANSPORTATION

1. Go to the Settings app on your phone.
2. To access the system navigation menu, go to System > Gestures.
3. Pick a choice:
   - No buttons: just gestures for navigation.
   - There are three buttons on the navigation bar: Home, Back, and The App Overview.
   - Pixel 3, 3 XL, 3a, and 3a XL all have two-button navigation, with Home and Back buttons.

Quickly navigate between different displays, websites, and applications

Return to

Return to the screen you were seeing before. Multiple visits are permitted. However, there is no way to return to any earlier screen when you reach the Home page.

- To use gesture navigation, just swipe horizontally or vertically from the screen's edges.
- Three-button navigation: Return to the previous screen.
- Pixel 3, 3 XL, 3a, and 3a XL, which all have 2 buttons: Tap Back.

Return to the main menu

- To navigate using gestures, swipe up from the screen's bottom.
- Three-button interface: Select Home.
- The Pixel 3, 3 XL, 3a, and 3a XL all have two-button navigation, which is to tap Home.

It's possible to have many Home screens. Access them by swiping to the right or left.

Determine which applications are currently running

- To navigate using gestures, swipe from the bottom, hold, and release.
- Select Overview from the three-button menu.
- Two-button interface (Pixel 3, 3 XL, 3a, and 3a XL): Swipe vertically from the screen's bottom to a central point.

It is possible to:

- Put an end to applications: Tap and hold the app icon.
- Run a program: Press the picture.
- Snap a picture: Click on Screenshot.
- Find the text in the languages you've chosen: To choose, use the Select button. After that, you may copy, share, or search the words on the app's picture by tapping on them.
- Keep an eye on two applications simultaneously.

You can't capture a screenshot or copy text from any open app while using the 2-button navigation.

Use different applications

- To use the gesture navigation, swipe left to right at the bottom of the screen.
- Select Overview from the three-button menu. Locate the desired app by swiping to the right. Press on it.
- For Pixel 3a and older, there is a two-button navigation: With a right swipe on Home, you may choose between your two most recent applications.

Click on Pixel Fold from the task bar

You may swiftly navigate between applications by tapping on their respective icons on the task bar.

- To access the task bar, swipe up from the bottom of the screen.
- The task bar will automatically collapse whenever you pick a new program.

Get access to every app

- Swipe up from the center or the bottom of your home screen to navigate using gestures.
- Swipe up from the center or the bottom of your home screen to get the three-button navigation.
- Two-button interface: From the center of your home screen, swipe up.

Phone search (Pixel 4a and later, Fold included)

You may use the search feature on your Pixel phone to find material on the web as well as on your Pixel device.

- Search results found on the web
- Applications: Apps and app-related material
- People: Everyone you know and the applications you use to stay in touch with them
- Configuration: Personalization of the phone, data, and functions
- App Store on Google Play: Play Store applications

- Images captured on the screen: Various images captured by your phone recently
- Google Assistant: Actions that may be performed inside the Assistant app to establish routines, communicate, and do other tasks
- Techniques for the Pixel Phone: unique hints, hacks, and updates for Pixel
  1. You may access the search bar on your phone by tapping on it or swiping it up from the bottom of the screen.
  2. Put in a search term, locate the result you're seeking, and then either touch on it to open it or scroll down to view additional results.

REARRANGE EVERYTHING

Choose or relocate objects

Choose by tapping

Tap the screen to choose or launch an app or other app on your phone. Pressing and holding text in certain applications brings up options to do things like play music or make a reservation.

Press and hold to enter the text

Just touch the area you want to text on to begin typing. There is a keyboard available for you.

Feel and grasp

Press and hold an on-screen object. Raise your finger once the object reacts.

Touch and hold an object to drag it. Navigate the screen with your fingertip without raising it. Raising your finger indicates that you have found the correct spot. To illustrate, you can reorganize your Home screen applications simply by dragging and dropping them.

Tap, drag, or tilt

Navigate the screen without stopping as quickly as possible. To access additional Home screens, for instance, you may swipe left or right on one.

Modify the position and size of objects

Alter the size with a double-touch

You may "zoom in" on some sites by tapping twice, such as a map or website.

To adjust the size, pinch and spread.

To modify the size of certain applications, you need to place two or more fingers on the screen. Put your fingers together in a pinch to constrict. To make them bigger, separate them.

Turn around

Most displays can follow your every move when you spin your phone. To activate or deactivate rotation, use a two-finger swipe from the top of the screen and touch the "Auto-rotate" button.

MAKE FAST ADJUSTMENTS TO YOUR SETTINGS

Quick Settings allows you to access and modify your settings without leaving any screen on your phone. You may add or relocate frequently used settings to the Quick Settings area for easy access.

Some of these instructions are only compatible with Android 11 and later.

LAUNCH INSTANT PREFERENCES

1. Swipe down from the top of the screen to get your initial configuration.
2. Again, swiping down will see all of your Quick Settings.

Enable or disable the settings

- Toggle the status of an option by tapping it. Your settings have been dimmed.
- Press and hold an option to bring up additional choices for that setting.

Make changes to, or delete a setting

- Press and hold the upper part of your screen for two seconds.
- Hit the Edit button located in the lower left corner.

Find the option and press and hold.

1. Choose the desired location by dragging the setting.
2. You can add a setting by dragging it up from "Hold and drag to add tiles."
3. Simply drag the setting to the "Drag here to remove" area to delete it.

Manage your video and audio with ease

You can adjust several settings for the media that is now playing, including pausing and rewinding. You can see what's playing on your phone by swiping down from the top.

Tip:

- If an app's icon isn't already there in your Quick Settings menu, you may be asked to add it. At any point, you have the option to delete or re-add these.
- When you have a lot of options enabled, your phone may conceal icons to make room on the screen. A dot will appear at the very top of your

phone's screen; tapping on it will reveal the concealed icons.

Master the sound and picture

- You can see what's playing on your phone by swiping down from the top.
- Pressing the panel will launch the app that plays the media.
- Swipe to the right or left to access your media apps if you're using more than one.
- To adjust the volume and position of your audio device, touch its name in the upper right corner of the panel. Like "Speakers" or "Pixel buds."

METHODS FOR RECORDING YOUR PHONE'S SCREEN

Methods for recording what's on your Google Pixel phone's screen and taking screenshots

Capture images (screenshots) or capture video from your Pixel phone's display. You may see, modify, and share the captured screencast once you've captured it.

Some of these instructions are only compatible with Android 11 and later.

TAKING A SCREENSHOT WITH YOUR PIXEL

1. Launch the application whose screen you want to record.
2. In the same motion, press the buttons labeled Power and Volume Down.
3. By default, your device will capture and save screen images.
4. You may see a preview of your screenshot in the lower left corner.

"Hey Google, take a screenshot" is another way to capture your screen.

Capture a screenshot while scrolling

These instructions are compatible with Android 12 and later versions, as well as the majority of displays that support scrolling.

1. Launch the application whose screen you want to record.
2. In the same motion, press the buttons labeled Power and Volume Down.
3. Press on Capture more located at the bottom.
4. Make advantage of the crop guidelines to choose the subject you want to capture.

Capture a screenshot devoid of buttons

Some interfaces allow you to capture screenshots even when no buttons are visible.

- Swipe up and hold from the screen's bottom to navigate using gestures. Pick a running program to capture a snapshot of. Click on Screenshot.
- 3-button interface: Press on Summary. Pick a running program to capture a snapshot of. Click on Screenshot.

LOCATING, SHARING, AND MODIFYING SCREENSHOTS

Select the preview of the screenshot you just took to access it.

Locating Every Single Screenshot

1. Launch Photos from your device.
2. The Tap Library Finally, screen captures.
   - Press the Share Share button to send a screenshot.
   - Press Edit Edit to make changes to a screenshot.

Tips for sharing your screen capture

Once you locate a screenshot you would want to share, just touch the Share Share button.

Editing a Screenshot: A Handy Guide

1. The Photos app is where you can locate your screenshot.
2. Click on Edit.

For Pixel 3 and after, including Fold, here's how to translate your screenshot:

The languages supported for screenshot translation are limited to:

- Chinese
- French
- German
- Hebrew
- Hindi
- Italian
- Korean
- Spanish
- Portuguese

1. Launch the app or website you want to translate on your mobile device.
2. Capture a screen capture.
3. Launch the Photos app from Google.
4. After choosing the desired screenshot, go to the Lens menu and choose Translate.

Steps to capture screen activity

1. Begin at the top of your screen and swipe down.

2. Select "Screen record."
   - To locate it, you may have to swipe to the right.
   - You may add screen recording to your Quick Settings by tapping Edit and dragging the option from there.
3. Press the Start button when you've decided what to record. Following the countdown, the recording will start.
   - Before beginning, you have the option to choose whether or not to record audio and display touches on the screen.
4. To end the recording, touch the screen recorder notice that appears when you scroll down from the top of the screen.

Locate screencasts

1. Launch Photos from your device.
2. Select Movies from the Library menu.

RETRIEVE AND REMOVE DATA FROM A PIXEL DEVICE

In most cases, the Files app on your Pixel phone will include all of your downloaded files.

- Android 10 and later are required to complete some of these procedures.

- Touching the screen is necessary for some of these procedures.

A PIXEL PHONE'S FILE SEARCH AND OPENING CAPABILITIES

1. Launch Files on your mobile device.
2. All of your file types will be visible.
3. Select a file type, then touch More, and finally choose Sort by to arrange files by name, date, or size.
4. A simple touch will open the file.

REMOVE DATA FROM YOUR GOOGLE PIXEL PHONE

1. Launch Files on your mobile device.
2. Before selecting a file, tap on a category.
3. Select Remove, and then Delete one file.

UPLOAD TO DRIVE, SHARE, PRINT, AND MORE

Let your Pixel phone serve as a file-sharing hub.

1. Caress and retain the file.
2. Press on Share.

Perform further operations, such as printing or transferring to Google Drive.

1. A simple touch will open the file.
2. Look for choices. For more options, click More.

DISCOVER A WIDE VARIETY OF MEDIA

There are a lot of applications that let you download things like books, movies, and music. You may access the material by navigating to the app from where you obtained it.

MOVE DATA TO A DESKTOP OR LAPTOP

To access the data stored on your device, just enter the "Downloads" folder on your computer after connecting your device to it via USB.

LIMIT YOUR SCREEN TIME ON YOUR PIXEL PHONE

Use Digital Wellbeing as a guide to limit your screen time on your Pixel phone.

Learn more about your Pixel phone habits, such as the average amount of time you spend in each app and the frequency with which you unlock it. Your digital wellness may be enhanced with the help of such information. You may plan to display changes and use app timers, for instance.

- Android 10 and later are required to complete some of these procedures.
- Touching the screen is necessary for some of these procedures.

ESTABLISH DIGITAL HEALTH

Simply open the Settings app on your device, go to Digital Wellbeing & parental controls, and then toggle the Show icon in the app list switch to make Digital Wellbeing appear like an app.

Digital Wellbeing requires you to create a profile the first time you use it.

1. Launch the Settings app on your smartphone.
2. Select Digital Wellbeing and set up parental restrictions.
3. Press and hold "More" until Oversee your data.

If you are the default parent account on a child's device, you may also control their account.

THE BEST APPS FOR TIME MANAGEMENT

Determine the amount of time you spend app-using.

1. Launch the Settings app on your smartphone.
2. Select Digital Wellbeing and set up parental restrictions.
3. Your device usage today is shown in the graphic. Tap the chart for more information. Take this case in point:
   - Regular screen time: How often you've unlocked your smartphone and launched

certain applications, as well as the duration of each app's display on the screen

- Alerts: The total number of alerts you've received and the applications that sent them
- Just touch on any of the apps to see additional details or adjust their settings.

4. Reduce the amount of time you spend on each app daily.

App timers may not be compatible with all work and school accounts.

1. Launch the Settings app on your smartphone.
2. Select Digital Wellbeing and set up parental restrictions.
3. Press the graph.
4. Select Set timer next to the app whose use you want to restrict.
5. Set a limit on how long you may use the app. Next, press the OK button.

When the timer runs out, the program will shut and the symbol will get darker. Remember that at midnight, all app timers reset.

- Remove the app timer by following steps 1-4 above if you want to use the app before midnight.

CONTROL HOW YOU USE GOOGLE CHROME

Determine the average amount of time you spend online.

1. Launch the Settings app on your smartphone.
2. Select Digital Wellbeing and set up parental restrictions.
3. Press on the graph Following that, Google Chrome.
   o Press the Show all applications button if you can't see it immediately.
4. Select Show sites after scrolling. Display follows. You can see which websites you frequented and for how long each day.
5. Click on it to get additional details about the time you've spent on a website.

Remove the history of site visits

Select the website from the list to hide your browsing history. Press the "Remove past visits" button. It will appear on the list once again when you visit the site at a later time.

Make a daily quotient for the amount of time you spend online.

1. Launch the Settings app on your smartphone.

2. Select Digital Wellbeing and set up parental restrictions.
3. Press on the graph Following that, Chrome.
   o Press the Show all applications button if you can't see it immediately.
4. Select "Set site timer" next to the desired restricted website.
5. Press OK after selecting a time limit.

BEDTIME MODE MIGHT HELP YOU SLEEP BETTER

Research snoring and coughing

Do not use the Digital Wellbeing app if you are pregnant or nursing. You should be able to use the knowledge to strike a balance using technology that works for you. See a doctor or nurse if you're worried about your health. Google makes no promises or representations about the efficacy of this feature.

You must have the most recent version of the Digital Wellbeing app to access this feature.

Use your phone's clock to see your data

1. Start the Clock app on your mobile device.
2. Make it bedtime.

- To enable Bedtime mode for the first time, go to the settings menu, find "Show cough and snore activity," and then touch Continue.

Attention all snorers and coughers! By tapping the Bedtime icon, you'll be able to toggle between the two activities.

Verify your information with Digital Wellbeing.

1. To access your phone's settings, open the app.
2. Turn on the parental controls and Digital Wellbeing.
3. Scroll down to "Show cough & snore activity" and then hit Continue.

Your cough and snoring data is located under "Bedtime mode" in your Digital Wellbeing app. Just launch the app the next time you want to see it.

Check all of your records

1. To access your phone's settings, open the app.
2. Just touch on Search up there.
3. Type in "cough."
4. Choose Cough & snore from the Digital Wellbeing app's menu.

Initiating a regular nighttime routine

1. Launch the Settings app on your smartphone.
2. Select Bedtime mode and then Bedtime routine from the Digital Wellbeing & parental settings menu.
3. You get to decide when the Bedtime mode turns on.
4. Use these two approaches to establish a nightly routine:
   - Establish a routine: Choose the days of the week you want to sleep in and the hours you want to go to bed.
   - Engage in charging mode: Charge your smartphone between the specified "After" and "Before" timeframes.

Make advantage of the fast settings to activate and deactivate Bedtime mode with ease.

Just for now, put those applications on hold.

1. Launch the Settings app on your device.
2. Select Focus mode from the Digital Wellbeing & parental controls menu.
3. You may suspend certain applications by selecting them. These applications will not work and will not send you alerts when Focus mode is active.
4. To block out all outside noise, go to Focus mode.

- Select Turn on immediately or Turn off now to toggle Focus mode on or off.
- By tapping + Set a timetable, you may program Focus mode to activate automatically.
- Tap Take a break and set a time limit to temporarily unpause applications while Focus mode is active.

Go to your device's Quick Settings and look for the option to add focus mode.

While walking, try not to get distracted (Pixel 2 and after).

By activating Heads Up, you will get helpful notifications to raise your gaze from your mobile device as you stroll around.

Start or stop Heads Up by doing:

1. Launch the Settings app on your smartphone.
2. Heads Up may be accessed via the Digital Wellbeing & parental controls screen.
   - Installing Heads Up is as simple as following the on-screen prompts.
   - Press the toggle next to "Heads Up" to disable Heads Up.

USE YOUR PHONE TO MAKE CONTACTLESS PURCHASES

At stores that use contactless payments, you can just tap and pay.

Some procedures are compatible with Android versions 11 and later.

DISABLE NEAR FIELD COMMUNICATION (NFC)

Warning: Near Field Communication (NFC) is not available on this phone. Contactless payments will not work.

1. Go to the Settings app on your phone.
2. Select NFC from the list of connected devices, then tap on Connection settings.
3. Toggle NFC on.

The Pixel Fold, like any other foldable smartphone, may be accessed via the tap-to-pay feature by folding it.

Direct applications that accept contactless payments

1. Verify that the option to pay using contactless is selected.

2. Launch the app that you want to use for touchless payments.
3. Go to the Settings app on your phone.
4. Select NFC from the list of connected devices, then tap on Connection settings.
5. Navigate to Payment default after tapping Contactless payments.
6. Assign a default payment app.

Your payment applications need to support contactless payments to appear in Settings. When it comes to contactless payments, money transfer applications aren't compatible. Google Play or the Play Store app on your mobile device may provide you with payment applications.

Use the power button to access your passes and cards.

When making contactless purchases using the Google Pay app, you'll be able to view all of your available payment methods and passes right on your home screen when you touch the power button. In the Settings app, you have the option to enable or disable cards and passes.

For the power button to unlock your cards and passes, you must have Google Pay installed and configured.

1. Launch the app called Settings.
2. Go to Gestures in the System menu, then tap Cards & Passes.
3. Toggle the switch for cards and passes.

Remove the obstacle to contactless payments caused by unwanted card readings.

If you're having trouble making contactless payments and your battery life is becoming short, try bringing your phone closer to a card or other object that has an NFC chip. Take a wallet-style phone cover with payment cards as an example. Take the case off and see whether it fixes the problem.

The near-field communication (NFC) sensor on your phone will persistently attempt to communicate with any nearby NFC-enabled object, such as a credit card.

Even if another cover seems to fit, it is still recommended that you choose a case made specifically for your phone's model.

BLOCK ALL CONTACTLESS PURCHASES
Disabling NFC will also disable any other functionality that relies on it.

1. Go to the Settings app on your phone.

2. Select NFC from the list of connected devices, then tap on Connection settings.
3. Forget about using NFC.

Launch your payment app and disable contactless payments if you like. Unfortunately, not all payment applications have this feature.

Discover the current musical lineup in your area

If you want to know more about the songs playing around you, you may ask your Pixel phone to recognize them.

- Notifications may be shown either while your phone is locked or when you are using it, depending on your preference.
- Even when your phone is locked, you may get additional music information by tapping the notification twice. On a mobile device, open the notifications section, swipe up to find the music notice, and then touch on it.
- In 2016, Pixel failed to recognize music.
- Android 10 and later are required to complete some of these procedures.
- Touching the screen is necessary for some of these procedures.

OBTAIN MUSIC DETAILS MECHANICALLY

Pixel (2016) isn't able to recognize music.

1. Go to the Settings app on your phone.
2. Select Now Playing from the Sound & vibration menu.
3. Locate local music by turning on the feature.
   - Check that your phone has enough juice and is linked to Wi-Fi.
4. Your phone will download the music database, so please be patient.
5. Once the download is complete, your lock screen will immediately display any songs that are currently playing in your immediate vicinity.
6. Find out more about a song by:
   - To unlock your phone, touch on the name of the music.
   - On a mobile device, open the notifications section, swipe up to find the music notice, and then touch on it.

Explore a wider range of songs with a music search

There is a lot of music that your phone can recognize automatically. You may always use Google's music search feature to find any songs it doesn't contain.

This function is only compatible with Pixel 4 and subsequent devices, including Fold.

1. Go to the Settings app on your phone.
2. Select Now playing from the Sound & vibration menu.
3. Permit the display of the search bar on the lock screen.
4. You have the option to search for music if your phone is unable to recognize it. Press the music search button on your lock screen to start searching for a song.

Recognize recently played music

1. Go to the Settings app on your phone.
2. Select Now Playing from the Sound & vibration menu.
   - The option to "Show songs on the lock screen" must be enabled.
3. Navigate to the history of what's now playing.
4. A playlist of all the music you've listened to will be shown.
5. Select a song to listen to it, share it, or play it in your music app. You may also choose numerous tracks to: on Pixel 3 and after, Fold included
   - Play on a streaming service
   - Send to others Remove from my contacts

- Which song did you like the most?

This function is compatible with Pixel 3a and subsequent models, including Fold.

From the convenience of your lock screen, you can effortlessly add any music currently playing nearby to your Now Playing favorites list.

Access the music note by tapping the icon next to the song title on your lock screen. A heart is then attached to the musical note. Tap the music note once again to de-favorite the song.

To analyze the music that you love:

1. Go to the Settings app on your phone.
2. Select Now Playing from the Sound & vibration menu.
3. Select Favorites from the Now Playing history.
4. Select a song to remove it from your favorites by tapping the red heart symbol.

MODIFY THE LOCATION OF ALERTS

You may disable the music notifications that appear at the top of your screen if you prefer not to receive them.

1. Go to the Settings app on your phone.

2. Press on Notifications, then on Now Playing, and last on Sound & vibration.
3. Disable the Acknowledged Music Notifications feature. You may still see song details on your lock screen.

The Game's Workings Right Now

In every Pixel phone

If music is playing nearby, your phone will attempt to identify the song by comparing a brief sample to its internal music library. The data processing that takes place on your phone is completely confidential.

To improve its song recognition, Now Playing gathers data such as the proportion of times it successfully identifies music. Now Playing will only gather this data if you have allowed Google to access your use and diagnostic data.

With federated analytics, on Pixel 4 and subsequent models (including Fold)

Pixel 4 and subsequent phones employ federated analytics, a privacy-preserving method, to aggregate the counts of songs identified and usage of the function. This will be used to enhance the Now Playing function and its song database, allowing it to identify the currently playing song more often. Google will never be able to tell which songs you like; all they can see are the global charts.

You may share the number of identified songs with Google if you've enabled shared use and diagnostics.

By using the "Show search button on lock screen" feature, Google can get a brief digital audio fingerprint for each search that you do, allowing it to identify audio content.

CHAPTER FIVE

LOCATE AND CONFIGURE NEARBY DEVICES

Your Pixel phone can locate nearby devices and allow you to set them up.

- Android 10 and later are required to complete some of these procedures.
- Feel free to use your fingertips on the screen for a few of these stages.

INSTALL NEW GADGETS WHEREVER YOU ARE

One must first set up their phone.

1. Now is the time to do it on your mobile device:
   - Then activate Bluetooth.
   - Open the Location app.
2. Remember to enable device alerts if you have already done so.

Get the new gadget ready for use.

Fast Pair-compatible devices, such as Chromecast, Wear OS watches, and other Android smartphones and tablets, may be set up. Discs labeled as compatible with quick pair are easy to spot. Some also include "Made for Google" or "Made by Google."

1. Press the power button on an unconfigured new gadget. Switch on the pairing mode on the device.
2. Power on your mobile device.
3. An invitation to install the new gadget will appear as a notification on your phone.
4. Press the alert.
5. Proceed as shown on the screen.

ACTIVATE OR DEACTIVATE ALERTS

You will automatically be notified about adjacent devices that you can configure. Even without alerts, you can see nearby devices in the Settings app on your phone.

1. Go to the Settings app on your phone.
2. Select Devices & sharing from the menu that appears after tapping Google.
3. On or off the "Scan for nearby devices" feature.

Get gadgets up and running again

- If you are unable to locate a notice, you may locate the device by navigating to the Settings app, selecting Google, and then selecting Devices & sharing.

- Inspect your proximity to the gadget. Fast Pair-compatible accessories must be within half a meter (1.6 feet) of your phone.
- Activate Bluetooth and Location Services on your mobile device.

Not all devices can be instantly found and set up by your phone. If the device you're trying to connect to isn't showing up in the Settings app, you may want to try using Bluetooth instead.

ZOOM IN USING PIXEL'S TOOL

The Pixel 5, Pixel Tablet, and Pixel Fold do not support this functionality at this time.

Use your phone's magnifying lens to see tiny prints, do intricate activities, or zoom in on distant signage. To increase contrast, you may also make use of visual effects. Your phone automatically adjusts the brightness when you take a picture in low light.

The Magnifier app may be downloaded.

You may get the Magnifier app from the Play Store on your Android device.

QUICKLY ACTIVATE THE MAGNIFIER

You may use the Magnifier app without first setting up Quick tap.

With a single swipe, you may quickly enable Magnifier:

1. Go to the Settings app on your phone.
2. Press System, followed by Gestures, and finally, Quick tap.
3. Enable the use of a quick tap.
4. Press on the Open app.
5. Find "Open app," then go to Settings, and last, Magnifier.
6. Pressing twice on the rear of your unlocked phone will launch Magnifier.

PINCH TO FOCUS

1. Switch on your phone's magnifying glass.
2. To zoom in on a certain topic, just aim your camera in that direction.
3. Gain and lose focus with the use of buttons or gestures:
   - Buttons: Pick the plus or minus sign next to the remove symbol at the bottom.
     You can find these on both sides of the Capture button.
   - Gestures: To zoom in or out on the picture, squeeze open or shut.
   - Feel free to swipe horizontally or vertically over the picture.

After taking a picture, you won't be able to use a horizontal or vertical swipe anymore; that feature is exclusive to the live view.

- Rotating from left to right enlarges the view while rotating from right to left decreases it.
- Both the bottom-to-top and top-to-bottom zoom modes are available.

You get a whopping 30x magnification on the Pixel 7 Pro and 8 Pro. With built-in image stabilization, your viewfinder's live picture will be automatically stabilized.

Put a picture on ice

To examine an enlarged picture in more depth, you have the option to freeze it.

1. Switch on your phone's magnifying glass.
2. Select Record. The picture you took stands still.
3. To examine the specific feature you want, just zoom in.

Your picture will be removed from the app after you exit.

- Hit the Download button to preserve it forever.
- You can find the downloaded picture in the Magnifier photo album, which is located at the bottom right of the screen.

- This gallery is only stored locally on your phone to ensure your privacy.
- Access the album in Google photographs, then toggle Back up on to begin backing up your photographs.
- You may hit the share symbol to send it to another messaging app.

CAPTURE BRIGHT IMAGES IN DIM LIGHTING

If the light is too dim, you may use the flashlight to see better.

1. Turn Off the Light by Tapping on the Light.
2. You may adjust the brightness using the slider.
   - The flashlight starts at its lowest level for stealth usage, and it automatically enhances low-light images when you freeze them using Magnifier.

RAISE OR LOWER THE BRIGHTNESS, CONTRAST, OR COLOR

In Magnifier, you may add effects to your photos by:

1. Switch on your phone's magnifying glass.
2. Find the "Show controls" option in the lower left corner.
3. You may adjust the brightness, contrast, and filters from the menu that appears.

- Press the Filters button to choose a color filter.

  You may choose the color of the filter by scrolling left or right.

  Eleven distinct color filters are at your disposal.

- To adjust the brightness of a picture, just tap on the Brightness button.
- Drag the slider to adjust the contrast.

4. You may customize a visual effect after tapping on it. Simply move the slider to the left or right.
   - If you want to add or remove items from the slider, tap the corresponding plus or minus sign.
   - To get your brightness and contrast levels back to how they were: Select Reset.
   - Returning to the previous filter: Choose "No filter" at the very top of the filter menu.

Unused filters may be hidden:

1. Press on Show controls in the lower left corner.
2. Press the "More settings" button.
3. Select Filters from the "Customization" menu.
4. To reveal certain filters, uncheck their boxes.
5. You may go back to the main menu by using the Back arrow.

Put the magnifying glass to use by holding it up to your eyes

A 5x mirror image is available with the help of Magnifier.

1. Switch on your phone's magnifying glass.
2. Press the Camera switch located at the bottom.
3. Adjust the magnification of your reflection.

MAKE USE OF YOUR PHONE'S MOVEMENTS

Hand gestures are a great way to control your phone. A few movements are toggleable.

- Android 10 and later are required to complete some of these procedures.
- Feel free to use your fingertips on the screen for a few of these stages.

TOGGLE THE USE OF GESTURES

1. Get into the Settings app on your phone.
2. Select Gestures from the System menu.
3. To modify a gesture, tap on it.

Research TalkBack gestures and magnification for accessibility gestures.

REVIEW ALERTS

1. Touch and hold to get alerts

To see your notifications on an unlocked Pixel phone with a fingerprint sensor, just swipe down on the sensor.

2. Select to view phone

A simple touch on the screen will reveal any alerts, even while your phone is locked.

3. Rise to examine the phone

Picking up your locked phone will allow you to see any alerts it has.

Rise to examine the phone

DISCOVER ALL OF THE APPLICATIONS YOU NEED

4. Locate popular app updates

   Drag from the bottom of the screen to the top, and then press and hold. Release when you sense a vibration.

5. Discover every app

   Raise your screen from the bottom by swiping it up.

Navigation by gestures

One-Tap access to frequently used apps and features

The Pixel 4a (5G) and subsequent phones are the only ones compatible with this function.

With only two presses on the rear of your phone, you may capture a screenshot or play and stop media. You may launch an app or display alerts. To modify your preferences:

1. Go to the Settings app on your phone.
2. Navigate to System > Gestures > Quick Tap.
3. Enable the use of a quick tap.
4. Pick an option.

- Choose "Open app" to launch an application. Next to "Open app," choose Settings. Finally, choose an app.

Just touch twice on the back of your phone to finish the activity.

Allow access to or change between cameras

- Immediately begin filming

  Pressing the power button twice on your phone will access the camera from any screen.

- Swivel lens

If you have your phone's camera app open, you may use two twists to toggle between the front and back cameras.

Twist twice to activate selfie mode

PUT THE PHONE ON SILENT IMMEDIATELY

- Choose between vibrating and silent.

  By simultaneously pressing the power and volume up keys, you may enable vibrating, mute, and silence the phone.

- For Pixel 2–4 only, squeeze to quiet.

The bottom part of your phone may be squeezed to reject timers, snooze alarms, and hush incoming calls.

Select Active Edge from the Gestures menu in your Settings app to adjust the squeezing pressure.

Gesture with your finger

- Change to "shhh"

Putting your phone facedown on a flat surface will activate Do Not Disturb mode rapidly.

Transform to silent

- Random noise (only Pixel 4 compatible)

Just one sweep of your hand over your phone can silence an incoming call, snooze an alarm, or disable a timer.

Interruptions caused by quiet

Enjoy some tunes (Pixel 4 supported only)

Just wave your hand over your phone to skip songs or return to the last one you were listening to.

CONSULT WITH YOUR ASSISTANT

- Use the corner to swipe

  To access Google Assistant while using gesture navigation, just swipe from the side of the screen to the right or left.

- Apply pressure on your screen (Pixel 2-4)

  Juxtapoz your phone's underside to access Google Assistant. To activate Google Assistant on Pixel 1 and 4a, just say "Ok Google."

  Go to your device's Settings, then System, Gestures, and finally Active Edge to adjust the squeezing pressure.

- Hold down the power button

To access Google Assistant on Pixel 6 and subsequent devices, just press and hold the Power button.

To access your Assistant with the Power button on Pixel 3 through Pixel 5a (5G), go into your device's settings:

1. Get into your phone's settings.
2. Navigate to System > Gestures.
3. Keep the Power button pressed.
4. Put the Assistant on Hold.

The Settings app is where you may adjust the duration of the press. Select System, and then Touch Controls. Following that, To power on, press and hold the button.

Gesture with your finger

MAKE YOUR PIXEL PHONE'S BATTERY LAST

If you take good care of your phone's battery and limit its drain, it will last longer throughout the life of the phone.

Some procedures are compatible with Android versions 11 and later.

As you use your Pixel device, the battery learns your habits and adjusts to maximize performance. It can take a few weeks for optimization to fully take effect after setting up a new device or doing a factory reset. Make sure to keep Adaptive Battery and Battery Optimization enabled for optimum performance.

PICK FOR BATTERY-SAVING SETTINGS

Modify the display of the computer

Dim the screen's illumination

1. Use two fingers to drag the screen from the top to the bottom.
2. To the left of the screen, you should see a slider.

Disable light theme

1. Go to the Settings app on your phone.
2. To get the dark theme, tap on Display.
3. Switch to the dark theme.

Mute the live wallpaper feature

Get more juice out of your battery by disabling live wallpapers.

When you're not using your screen, be sure to turn it off.

1. Go to the Settings app on your phone.
2. To lock the screen, tap on Display.
3. When you're not using your screen, be sure to turn it off:
   - The Google Pixel 4: To turn off the idle lock screen, tap on it.
   - Every pixel: Turn off Keep all information up-to-date.

Allow your screen to power down earlier

1. Go to the Settings app on your phone.
2. Select Screen timeout from the Display menu.
3. Choose duration, say 30 seconds.

The Pixel 4 lets you set a brief screen timer and have the screen remain on while you gaze at it. Launch the Settings app on your phone and then choose Display. Following that, Select "Screen attention" and then toggle it on.

Offset Smooth Display (Pixel 4 and later, Fold included)

1. Get into the Settings app on your phone.
2. To smooth the display, tap Display.
3. Put Smooth Display on pause.

Allow the screen's brightness to adjust on its own

1. Go to the Settings app on your phone.
2. To get adaptive brightness, tap on Display.
3. Adjust the light level to your liking.

Adjust the connection settings (Pixel 4a (5G) and later, including Fold)

Adaptive connection may be restricted by some US carriers. To find out more, call your cellular provider.

1. Get into the Settings app on your phone.
2. Select Adaptive connection from the Network & internet menu.
3. Adjust the level of adaptive connection.

CUT DOWN ON IDLE POWER US

(Only Pixel 4 users may turn off Motion Sense)

If you want to conserve power on your Pixel 4, you may disable its ambient light sensor.

Quit labeling music

To save power, disable Now Playing, which detects nearby music and plays it automatically.

Limit battery-intensive applications

Prevent programs from using a lot of battery power in the background

1. Go to the Settings app on your phone.
2. Click on the Battery icon.
3. Press the message, and then choose Restrict, if it suggests blocking a specific program or system.

Limit the use of applications that drain the battery quickly.

1. Go to the Settings app on your phone.
2. To access battery consumption, tap on Battery.
   - To see how much power each app uses, choose View by applications.
3. Select an app or system to see its battery use details or to make changes. It is highly recommended that you enable battery optimization for all applications.
   - Restricting background battery use is possible for some programs.
   - If you want to see how each app uses battery life:
4. Go to the Settings app on your phone.
   - Click on Apps, and then Power consumption of the app.

When you set some applications to "Restricted," you could notice that they don't perform properly or that alerts are delayed.

Continue to use the adaptive battery

Enable your phone's adaptive battery feature.

1. Go to the Settings app on your phone.
2. Select Adaptive options after tapping Battery.
3. Saddle up the Adaptive Battery.

Unplug features that use a lot of power

- When you're not making use of them, disable tethering and hotspots.
- Avoid having your Wi-Fi activated when you're in range of a network you've stored.

Ruling out unneeded user profiles

Saving power on a phone is possible with fewer accounts. The owner of the phone can remove user profiles and accounts.

BATTERY MAINTENANCE IS ESSENTIAL

Put your phone's original power adapter to use.

There are other power adapters and chargers that may charge slowly, if at all. Plus, they pose a threat to the battery or phone.

Remain calm

Stay away from places where your phone could become too hot.

Even while not in use, a heated battery will drain much more quickly. Your battery may be damaged by this kind of discharge.

Don't leave your phone plugged in for longer than necessary since it will warm up.

You may set your prices.

It is not necessary to educate your phone on the battery's capacity by charging it from full to zero or vice versa.

The Adaptive Charging Process (Pixel 4 and Later, Fold Included)

Adaptive Charging ensures that your phone charges to 100% an hour before you disconnect it from the charger, which is useful when charging for an extended period or overnight. You can extend the life of your battery using the Adaptive Charging option. Phones that support this functionality are:

- When you charge your Pixel 4 from 9 PM to 4 AM and have an alarm set for 3-10 AM, it will turn on.

- Pixel 4a and subsequent models, among Fold: Your charging patterns are learned via the Adaptive Charging function. Despite the aforementioned circumstances, it may still activate if a lengthy charging session is anticipated.

This function takes around 14 days to understand how you typically charge your device. While you're away from home, for example, Adaptive Charging may not activate.

Stop Adaptive Charging by doing:

1. Get into the Settings app on your phone.
2. Select Battery, followed by Adaptive Charging.
3. Disable the Adaptive Charging feature.

A notice will show you when your battery will be completely charged when you switch on Adaptive Charging.

Keeping your battery life extended (Pixel 3 and later, Fold included)

Note that Android 11 and later are the only ones that support this capability.

Under some circumstances, your phone will automatically restrict charging to about 70% to 80%

to preserve the health of your battery and help it last longer. These scenarios include:

- Charging indefinitely at high temperatures for more than a few hours
- Nonstop power for quite a few days

A message reading "Protecting your battery" will appear whenever this function is enabled. "Charging optimized to protect your battery" is another statement that appears in the Settings app under Battery.

This function is disabled immediately whenever the phone doesn't match the requirements mentioned above. When the phone begins to charge to 100%, you'll know that the function is off.

To disable the battery saver and allow the phone to charge to 100%, either restart your Pixel phone or go to the Settings app and find the "Battery" section. Tap on the "Charge to full" option.

Whenever your phone satisfies the aforementioned requirements, this function will be activated immediately.

DOWNGRADE YOUR MOBILE DATA USE USING DATA SAVER

Turning on Data Saver might help you use less mobile data on a restricted plan. Most applications and services may access background data only over Wi-Fi in this mode. Services and applications that are now running may access mobile data.

Android 8.0 and later are required to complete some of these tasks.

ENABLE OR DISABLE DATA SAVER

1. Go to the Settings app on your phone.
2. Choose "Network & internet." Next, we have Data Saver.
3. Toggle the switch for Data Saver.
   - The Data Saver symbol will appear in your status bar when Data Saver is enabled.
   - The Settings app on your phone will also display a notice at the top.

The settings bar is a good place to find Data Saver.

Maintain uninterrupted app use even when Wi-Fi is unavailable.

Allowing some programs and services to operate in the background when you're not using them is necessary for them to function properly. By enabling

173

"Unrestricted data" for certain applications, you may enable background app use of mobile data.

1. Go to the Settings app on your phone.
2. To access unrestricted data, go to Network & internet, then data saver.
3. To begin using mobile data when Data Saver is on, launch the app or service you want to utilize.

NIGHTTIME SCREEN CUSTOMIZATION ON PIXEL

Changing the screen's color settings might help your phone last longer on a single charge and make it easier to see in low light. If you're having trouble falling asleep when using your phone at night, try switching to the Dark theme, Night Light, or Grayscale.

You'll need Android 9.0 or later to complete some of these tasks.

Turn your phone's wallpaper and applications black automatically.

By enabling the Dark theme, you can reduce the brightness of your phone's backdrop. Nightly activation of the Dark theme may be programmed.

Your phone's battery life may be extended when you utilize applications that are compatible with the Dark theme. When it comes to battery life, apps that aren't compatible with the Dark theme are useless. Additionally, disabling location services will render sunset-to-dawn scheduling ineffective.

1. Go to the Settings app on your phone.
2. To get the dark theme, tap on Display.
3. Press on the Schedule button.

Choose between three options: turn on at a certain time, from sunset till dawn, or when you go to bed.

If you have an Android device running 13 or later, you may set Bedtime mode to automatically activate the Dark theme.

1. Go to the Settings app on your phone.
2. To get the dark theme, tap on Display.
3. Select Turns on at Bedtime from the Schedule menu.

Go to Schedule > None to disable automatic Dark theme activation.

Be sure Bedtime mode is functioning correctly by doing the following:

1. Keep your Digital Wellbeing app up-to-date.

2. Just go into your phone's Settings and toggle on the "Digital Wellbeing" alerts.

You may access the Night Light, Bedtime mode, and Dark theme using your phone's Quick Settings.

DIM THE BACKGROUND OF YOUR PHONE AUTOMATICALLY

The wallpaper will be dimmed when the battery saver is turned on.

You may set your phone's wallpaper to a lower brightness when you go to sleep on Android 13 and later.

1. Go to the Settings app on your phone.
2. Press the option for Digital Wellbeing and parental controls.
3. Choose the "Bedtime Mode" screen.
4. Embed the Bedtime Mode.
5. Then, choose "Customize." Things to do on screens before bed.
6. Enable Low Wallpaper Lightness.

Set your screen to a warm amber or night light mode automatically.

You may adjust the blue tone of your screen to make it more readable in low light. If you have trouble falling asleep, try avoiding blue light. With Night

Light, you can easily adapt your eyes to night vision by turning your screen red or amber.

1. Go to the Settings app on your phone.
2. Access the night light by tapping the display.
3. Press Schedule to choose the beginning and ending times.
   - Press Turns on at custom time to set a custom time for turning on. After that, provide the "Start time" and the "End time."
   - To activate it from dusk to dawn, just touch the corresponding button. If location services are disabled, sunset-to-dawn scheduling will not function.

Select None from the Schedule menu to disable the automatic activation of night mode.

SWITCH TO GRAYSCALE MODE AUTOMATICALLY

Grayscale, which turns your phone's screen to black and white, might help you relax at night.

1. Go to the Settings app on your phone.
2. Press the option for Digital Wellbeing and parental controls.
3. Press the "Bedtime" button.
4. Go to sleep mode.

- To access this option on Android 13 and later, choose Settings, and then Things to do on screens before bed.
5. Saddle up with grayscale.

You may access the Night Light, Bedtime mode, and Dark theme using your phone's Quick Settings.

MAKE YOUR THEME CHANGES

You have complete control over the settings and may toggle the themes on and off whenever you like.

1. Go to the Settings app on your phone.
2. Select Screen.
3. Press the color selection on your screen:
   - Toggle the Dark theme on the "Appearance" screen.
   - In the "Color" section, toggle the flashlight on.

CHAPTER SIX

FIND, LAUNCH, AND DISMISS APPLICATIONS

You can access all of your applications in the All applications section, and some of them will be on your Home screens. Launch applications, navigate between them, and even locate two apps simultaneously.

You'll need Android 9.0 or later to complete some of these tasks.

Locate and launch applications

Accessible from any location

1. Drag the screen's bottom edge toward the top.
2. Select the desired app by tapping on it.

The "Work" tab is where you'll discover all of your applications if you're using your Google Account for school or work.

Starting with

1. To open the app, press and hold.
2. Pick one option if you have one.

Starting from the Home Screen

1. Drag the screen's bottom edge toward the top.
   - Just put the app's name into the Search field to launch it.
2. Browse recently used applications
3. Pull up from the bottom, press down, and release.

On Android Go, you may access recent applications by tapping the three-button menu.

1. To launch a different app, just swipe left or right.
2. Select the desired app by tapping on it.

Sliding the Home button to the right is another method to switch.

On the main menu (Pixel Fold only)

Pressing an app's icon on the task bar allows you to swiftly move between applications.

- The task bar may be accessed by swiping up from the bottom of the screen.
- The task bar will automatically collapse whenever you pick a new program.

Put an end to programs

- Turn off one app: Pull up from the bottom, press down, and release. Pull up the app.
- Power off all applications: Pull up from the bottom, press down, and release. Use a left-to-right swipe. Tap on Clear all on the left.
- Put an end to all Android applications Go: Drag from the bottom to the top, then release. Select Clear all located at the bottom.
- Navigate to your home screen: Select "Home" from the menu.
- Turn off background processes in all of your apps:
  1. Swipe down twice from the top of the screen to enter Quick Settings.
  2. Find the total number of background processes by tapping the #active applications icon in the bottom left.
     - Alternately, you may touch the corresponding number next to Settings and Power from the bottom right.
     - Press the Stop button to exit any open app.

You won't drain the power or memory even if you don't close applications. This is handled automatically by Android.

Discover brand-new applications

The Google Play app is where you may find other applications.

Select an aspect ratio for your applications (only to Pixel Fold)

Unfortunately, not all applications are made to accommodate the Pixel Fold screen. You may adjust the aspect ratio of an app to make it seem better on your screen. Aspect ratios may only be changed by individual apps.

1. Get into the Settings app on your phone.
2. Select the Aspect ratio (experimental) from the Apps menu.
3. Click on "Suggested apps" and then Browse all applications to see what's installed on your phone.
4. Select the app whose aspect ratio you want to modify.
5. Pick a ratio for the picture:
   - Application initialization: Launch the app at the standard size.
   - Expand the program to occupy the whole screen.
   - The program occupies only half of the screen.

Changing the aspect ratio may cause the program to restart, so save your work before proceeding. Certain applications just don't work well with specific aspect ratios.

MANAGE YOUR DEFAULT APPLICATIONS

You may set the default app to use if you have many apps that perform the same function. For instance, you may pick and choose which of your photo editing applications to launch when you want to edit a picture.

You'll need Android 9.0 or later to complete some of these tasks.

Make certain applications the default on your phone.

Select the option when prompted

1. Select the desired app by tapping on your screen if prompted to do so by your mobile device.
2. Determine how often you would want to do this task using that app: Once in a while or always.
   - Your smartphone will no longer prompt you to choose an app to perform that activity if you choose Always.
   - Cleaning the default will force your device to ask again.

Determine when to choose

1. Navigate to the Settings app on your respective smartphone.
2. Select Default applications from the applications menu.
3. Select the default setting that you want to modify.
4. To set an app as your default, touch on it.

Reset your phone to the factory settings of an app.

1. Navigate to the Settings app on your respective smartphone.
2. Open the Apps menu.
3. You may change the default app by tapping on it. To access it, go to the App details or See the All Applications menu.
4. Turn on Open automatically.
5. You may disable Open supported links.

Your smartphone will prompt you to choose an app the next time you clear the default.

APP PERMISSIONS MAY BE CHANGED

Some applications may request access to your device's resources, such as the camera or contact list before you permit them. You may choose to Allow or Deny an app's request to access your device's capabilities when you get a notice about it. In the settings of your device, you have the option to adjust permissions for all apps or certain types of rights.

Some procedures are compatible with Android versions 11 and later.

MODIFY THE APP'S ACCESS RIGHTS

1. Navigate to the Settings app on your Smartphone.
2. Open the Apps menu.
3. To change an app, touch on it. Touch See all applications if it's not visible. Pick an app thereafter.
4. Select Permissions.
   - You can see the app permissions you granted or rejected here.
5. Select Allow or Don't Allow from the drop-down menu to modify a permission option.

There are a few options you could have when it comes to location, camera, and microphone permissions:

- Whenever: Just for the sake of place. Even when you're not actively using the app, it may still utilize the permission.
- Just when you're using the app, enable: You must be actively using the app for it to be able to utilize the permission.
- Never miss an opportunity to ask: The app will prompt you to utilize the permission each time you launch it. It may continue to utilize the permission as long as you continue to use the app.
- Do not permit: Even when you're using the app, it won't be able to utilize the permission.

ALTER ACCESS LEVELS ACCORDING TO THEIR CLASSIFICATION

Locate the applications that have the same permissions by using this feature. If you want to see which applications can see your calendar, you can do that.

1. Navigate to the Settings app on your Smartphone.

2. Select Permission Manager from the Security & Privacy menu. Then, tap on Privacy.

3. Press on a certain kind of allowance.

   - This is where you can see the applications for which you have granted or refused permission.

4. You may modify an app's permissions by tapping on it and then going to the settings menu.

MANY FORMS OF AUTHORIZATION

Phones might have different settings.

Listed here are the various app permissions and the actions they do when enabled.

- Access data about your vital signs from your body's sensors.
- Schedule: View your schedule.
- Access and edit your phone's call log.
- Capture images and capture video using the camera.
- Users: Get access to your user contacts.
- Files: Manage all of your device's files with ease.
- Get a hold of where your smartphone is at all times.
- Microphone: Capture sound.

- Listen to music and play audio files stored on your smartphone.
- Locate, link, and ascertain the relative location of devices nearby.
- Messages: Communicate messages.
- Phone: Handle incoming and outgoing calls.
- Media files: View media files stored on your mobile device.
- Physical exercise: Keep track of your steps, distance walked, speed, and other forms of physical activity.
- Communicate via short messaging service (SMS) and read sent SMS messages.

Unused app permissions should be automatically removed.

1. Navigate to the Settings app on your Smartphone.
2. Open the Apps menu.
3. To change an app, touch on it.
   - Touch See all applications if it's not visible. Pick an app thereafter.
4. Click the "Unused app settings" button and enable the feature to pause the app while it's not in use.

APPS MAY BE DOWNLOADED ON THE PIXEL PHONE

Google Play is an app store where Android users may download both free and paid applications for their mobile devices. While Google Play is where we advise you to obtain applications, there are other options.

Google Play Protect is a built-in security feature on Android devices that scans for and, if found, deletes applications that might be detrimental to your device.

Android 8.0 and later are required to complete some of these tasks.

APPS MAY BE FOUND ON GOOGLE PLAY

1. Launch Google Play.
   - Google Play is an app you may install on your mobile device.
   - Access play.google.com from your desktop or laptop.
2. Get the app of your choice.
3. See what other users have to say about the app to be sure it's trustworthy.
   - You can see the number of downloads and star ratings just under the app's name.

189

- Keep scrolling until you reach the "Ratings and Reviews" area to read specific reviews.
4. To install an app, either touch the pricing (for paid applications) or the Install button (for free apps).

Make Google Play aware of any problematic applications.

Tell us about any app that you feel might cause damage.

GET APPLICATIONS FROM SOMEWHERE ELSE

Your phone and personal data are vulnerable to app security threats posed by untrusted sources.

- Accidental damage or data loss might occur on your phone.
- Potential damage or hacking to your personal information exists.

Find other places to get applications

1. Get the program started downloading from the other source.
2. Just do what it says on the screen. Tap on "OK And" and then "Install" if prompted to do so by the source.

3. From the pop-up window that appears, choose Settings.
4. Approve requests from this source.

Stop installing programs from unknown sources.

1. Go to the Settings app on your phone.
2. Select Apps, then Select Special App Access, and finally, Install Unknown Apps.
3. Press the icon of the app you want to disable the option to install third-party applications.
4. Make this source's Allow feature inactive.

Give Google a hand in preventing malicious applications from third parties.

Your phone may communicate with Google about applications installed from sources other than Google Play.

This data helps Google in its efforts to safeguard users from malicious applications. Details like IP addresses, device IDs, Android versions, and app-related URLs might be among the pieces of data collected.

USE YOUR PIXEL OR TABLET TO SNAP A SELFIE

Your Pixel device's front-facing camera allows you to capture selfies.

SWITCH UP YOUR PERSPECTIVE

1. Slide open the Google Camera app.
2. Push the Switch button to switch to your front-facing camera.
3. Select Record.

An alternative to using buttons to rotate the lens for a selfie is:

1. Get your gadget twisted so it spins counterclockwise.
2. Reverse the process to turn the lens around.

Pick a method for saving selfies

Both mirrored and non-mirrored versions of your selfies may be saved. After taking a selfie, it won't seem flipped if you save it as a preview.

You may toggle the selfie-mirroring feature on and off in the camera by tapping the down arrow at the top and then selecting Settings. To save the selfie as shown, tap the saved image.

To alter the look of a selfie

Fix a selfie

Portrait mode and selfies are both compatible with face editing.

1. Use the down arrow to apply filters to a portrait or selfie shot.
2. The section titled "Face Retouching" includes:
   - Coming soon: Pixel 4a (5G) and beyond Tap on Soft or Smooth.
   - Pixel 4a and older models: Select Smooth or Natural.

Tip: The final shot is the only one that displays the outcomes of the face editing.

Get a better selfie

You have to go to the front-facing camera first before you can adjust the brightness of selfies. Using the down arrow and the Selfie Illumination option will make your selfies brighter.

Take a closer look at your selfie (Pixel 3 only)

With the Pixel 3, you can take selfies with a wider angle of view thanks to its ultra-wide front camera. Use the slider on the screen's bottom before taking a selfie to increase the number of individuals who can fit in the shot.

SIMPLIFY SELFIE-TAKING WITH VOICE COMMANDS

To take a selfie, Guided Frame will let you know when you're in the frame. A dotted frame encircles your face, and vibrations and spoken instructions let you know when to snap the shot.

Enable TalkBack to access Guided Frame.

1. Navigate to the Settings app on your respective smartphone.
2. To access TalkBack, tap on Accessibility.
3. You may toggle Use TalkBack on and off.

Open the Google Camera app to begin using Guided Frame:

1. Hold down the button on your front-facing camera.
2. Pressing the front camera button twice will activate the selfie mode.
3. Pay attention to the vibrations or hear the instructions.
4. Your selfie is captured by the Camera app.

Use your hands-free selfie stick

Use the following to snap a selfie without using your hands on your Pixel device:

- Photo timer.
- Timer for palm.
- Digital Personal Assistant by Google.

CAPTURE A SELF-PORTRAIT USING THE TIMER

To use the timer to snap a selfie:

1. Launch the software known as Google Camera.
2. From the menu bar, choose Settings.
3. Select between three or ten seconds on the "Timer" interface.
4. To begin the countdown on the timer, press the Capture button.

Use your hand to start a selfie timer (Pixel 6 and later models)

If you want to take a selfie while holding your Pixel Fold or Tablet:

1. Launch Google Camera. The Google Camera.
2. To begin the countdown, just raise your hand in front of the camera when your device's camera timer is turned on.

3. Before you start using the Palm timer, get your face in the shot.
   - The camera can see that your palm is looking straight forward.
   - Your hand and face are both visible.

SPEAK YOUR WAY INTO A SELFIE

With Google Assistant, you can snap a picture without using your hands on your Pixel smartphone.

To snap a picture without using your hands:

1. Launch Google Camera. The Google Camera.
2. Position your gadget so it can't fall or shake.
3. Get out of the way and into the shot.
   - A voice command to activate the camera's timer is "OK, Google, take a picture." A picture will be captured by your phone after a three-second pause.

CAPTURE DYNAMIC SHOTS USING TOP SHOT

Using Top Shot, you may choose your best still image or moving video clip from your motion picture shoot.

You may capture action pan or long exposure photos by switching to motion mode.

Neither the Pixel 7a nor the Pixel Fold support Action Pan.

1. Launch Google Camera.
2. Find "Motion"; scroll down.
3. Make your selection for the blur effect:
   - Action Plan: Give the backdrop a unique blur. If you want to get creative with blurring the backdrop, hold the camera motionless or follow a moving topic. Once you're satisfied with the shot, tap the Capture button.
   - Using a long exposure, you may artistically blur a moving scene. To get a creative blur effect, either keep the camera stationary or follow a moving subject. Once you're satisfied with the shot, tap the Capture button.

   The choice between Action Pan and Long Exposure

Device	Action Pan	Long Exposure
Pixel 5a (5G) and earlier	No	No
Pixel 6	Yes	Yes
Pixel 6 Pro	Yes	Yes
Pixel 6a	No	No
Pixel 7	Yes	Yes
Pixel 7 Pro	Yes	Yes
Pixel 7a	No	Yes
Pixel Fold	No	Yes

Advice for getting the most out of your Action Pan shots:

- A face-recognizable human being is the topic.
- The topic is changing. Low- or no-motion effect may be seen in photographs of stationary or very sluggish subjects.
- One primary topic stands out. Always aim to have your subjects stand out from the background by placing them firmly in the front.
- The subject occupies a significant portion of the shot and has been in the viewfinder for over a second before pressing the capture button.

Instructions on How to Take a Long-Exposure Shot

Keeping your gadget still is ideal for Long Exposure. Pressing the Capture button initiates the long exposure mode.

Depending on the size and speed of the object in focus, the exposure time adjusts to capture any motion in the image.

You may extract still images from a moving movie or photograph using Top Shot.

You may get suggestions for a higher-quality Top Shot when you shoot a short video or snapshot.

You must have a Pixel 3 or later, or the Pixel Fold, to access these features.

MAKE TOP SHOT ACTIVE

1. Start the Camera app on your mobile device.
2. Press Settings in the lower left corner.
3. Turn the Top Shot on or set it to auto-play.

An easy way to receive assistance with taking motion images on your Pixel 8 or Pixel 8 Pro is to activate Google Assistant and ask, "How do I take motion photos?"

TAKE A GREAT PICTURE

Using Top Shot, you may choose your best still image or moving video clip from your motion picture shoot.

HDR and greater resolution are the default settings for recommended images.

Press More, then Export, Video, and finally Export to save the moving picture as a video.

TOGGLE THE USE OF FREQUENT FACES

Pixel 4 and subsequent devices, including Fold, include an improved camera that can learn which faces you shoot or film most often and then suggest ways to improve those photos.

Your camera learns which photographs include the faces you shoot often and suggests more like them while you're taking still images or short movies. After that, your camera will suggest more flattering shots of those faces.

When you enable Frequent Faces, your camera will remember information about the faces you capture. Your smartphone will save all facial data, not Google. Your data will be erased if you deactivate Frequent Faces.

To activate Frequent Faces:

1. The slide opens the Google Camera app.
2. To access further options, go to the bottom left and hit options.
3. Click on the Faces You See Most Often.
4. Make the Faces feature active.

Frequent Faces is a game-changer when it comes to how your camera captures skin tones.

USE YOUR PIXEL WITH AUGMENTED REALITY

You may use your Pixel phone's Camera app to explore augmented reality. Photos and movies may both be enhanced using augmented reality (AR).

Create an AR picture using tools like Playmoji, AR stickers, or the Playground.

Playground is exclusive to the Pixel 4 and older models. Pixel 3, Pixel 3a, and Pixel 4 are the only devices that support Playmoji.

To capture images that include people and props:

1. Launch Google Camera. The Google Camera.
2. Move to Playground by tapping More.
3. Navigate to Playmoji or Stickers by tapping on Stickers.
   - Emojis are animated GIFs.
   - Stickers are two-dimensional figures.
4. Choose a sticker or Playmoji.
   - Hit Install to get the latest Playmoji.
5. You can move a sticker or Playmoji around by touching and holding onto it. Selfies include animated figures that can move and respond independently. You may also change the animations or add text to your screen.

- Substitute language: Select Text.
- Make anything smaller or larger: Give the item a tap. Next, squeeze your fingers together or apart.
- Take something out: Drag an item to the upper right, towards Delete, after touching and holding it.
- View an alternative assortment: Select Decal.
6. Pull down the camera shutter button.

To exit Playground, use the Come button.

CREATE A VIRTUAL REALITY FILM

Playground is exclusive to the Pixel 4 and older models. Pixel 3, Pixel 3a, and Pixel 4 are the only devices that support Playmoji.

To record footage with moving subjects and props:

1. Launch Google Camera. The Google Camera.
2. Move to Playground by tapping More.
3. Navigate to Playmoji or Stickers by tapping on Stickers.
    - Emojis are animated GIFs.
    - Stickers are two-dimensional figures.
4. Choose a sticker or Playmoji.
    - Hit Install to get the latest Playmoji.
5. You can move a sticker or Playmoji around by touching and holding onto it. Selfies include

animated figures that can move and respond independently. You may also change the animations or add text to your screen.

- Substitute language: Select Text.
- Make anything smaller or larger: Give the item a tap. Next, squeeze your fingers together or apart.
- Take something out: Drag an item to the upper right, towards Delete, after touching and holding it.
- View an alternative assortment: Select Decal.
6. Hold down the Capture button to start recording a video.

To exit Playground, use the Come button.

USE YOUR PIXEL PHONE TO CAPTURE VIDEO

Your mobile device can record both in slow motion and in real-time. Another option is to capture time-lapse films, which, when played back, will accelerate.

- Android 10 and later are required to complete some of these procedures.
- Feel free to use your fingertips on the screen for a few of these stages.

MAKE A RECORDING

Just so you don't miss a thing, when you record a video your phone will automatically turn off all alerts.

Press and hold capture in the Google Camera app to swiftly capture a video.

1. Launch Google Camera. The Google Camera.
2. To change from Photo to Video mode, press the video button. Go into video mode.
3. To begin recording, press the Record button.

- You may pause your video by using the Pause button. Again, press Record to begin recording.
- Press the Capture button to snap a high-resolution picture even while you record a movie.

4. Tap Stop to stop recording.

You can access tools like flashes and gridlines by adjusting your camera's settings.

Apply visual effects

Smooth out a video (Pixel 3a and later)

1. Slide open the Google Camera app.
2. To change from Photo to Video mode, press the video button. Go into video mode.

3. Press Video Settings, followed by Stabilization, located in the lower left corner.
4. Pick the stabilizing method that best suits your needs.
   - Select Standard to record the movement of light.
   - Just the Pixel 4a (5G) and newer models: To snap still images, press the Locked button.
   - Just the Pixel 4a (5G) and newer models: To record vigorous motion, use the Active button.
5. The amount of stabilization may be changed for each mode.

Pixel 7 and Pixel 7 Pro users may access cinematic video effects.

You may maintain topic focus while blurring the backdrop in Cinematic mode. If you want to use Cinematic mode:

1. Launch Google Camera on your mobile device.
2. Before you start filming, make sure you're not in Camera mode. Go into video mode.
3. Tap to activate the Cinematic Blur mode.
4. Pull the trigger to start recording.
5. To concentrate on a certain topic, tap on it.

Pixel 7 and Pixel 7 Pro users may enjoy vivid video colors.

Vibrant video color is captured while shooting in high dynamic range (HDR). Enabling 10-bit HDR video requires:

1. Launch Google Camera. The Google Camera.
2. To change from Photo to Video mode, press the video button. Go into video mode.
3. Press Video Settings in the lower left corner.

With the Pixel 7 and Pixel 7 Pro, you can capture high-definition video with any lens and up to 60 frames per second in 4K. If you want to enable high-definition video:

1. Launch Google Camera. The Google Camera.
2. Before you start filming, make sure you're not in Camera mode. Go into video mode.
3. Press Video Settings in the lower left corner.
   - Scroll down to "Resolution" and toggle it to 4K.
   - Adjust the frame rate to 60 frames per second.

Obtain a slow-motion recording.

To capture a slow-motion video:

1. Launch Google Camera. The Google Camera.

2. To change from Photo to Video mode, press the video button. Go into video mode.
3. Turn the speed down.
4. To begin recording, press the Record button.
   - Press the Capture button to snap a high-resolution picture while you record a slow-motion film.
5. Tap Stop to stop recording.

Using 1/8x as a guide, you can capture very fast speeds in slow motion.

Get some time-lapse footage.

To document gradual changes, such as a sunset:

1. Launch Google Camera. The Google Camera.
2. To change from Photo to Video mode, press the video button. Select Time Lapse from the video mode menu.
3. Select Auto from the options for the speed-up timer in the lower right.
4. Choose a speed setting. Just to illustrate:
   - Tap five times to skip 10 seconds of the video and 50 seconds of reality.
   - Tap 120 times to skip 10 seconds of the video, which takes 20 minutes in real life.
5. Select Record.

- Press the Capture button to snap a high-resolution picture while you film a time-lapse.
6. Tap Stop to stop recording.

Hit Auto if you don't know the speed to use or for how long to record.

For Time Lapse Night Sight to be enabled:

1. Launch Google Camera. The Google Camera.
2. To change from Photo to Video mode, press the video button. Select Time Lapse from the video mode menu.
3. Select Settings from the menu on the left side, and then choose More Light.
4. Press the Night Sight icon.
5. Select Record. While the phone captures the video, keep it steady.
6. Tap Stop to stop recording.

Create a virtual reality film

With the Pixel phone, you can also record augmented reality videos.

GET THE MOST OUT OF VIDEO BOOST ON PIXEL

This capability will be made available to Pixel 8 Pro customers in stages starting from December 7, 2023. You may have to wait a little.

The Pixel phone allows you to record films with superior lighting, colors, and details.

Video Boost needs Google Photos to analyze and back up videos.

HOW TO USE VIDEO BOOST

One must first activate Video Boost and then capture a video.

1. The slide opens the Google Camera app.
   - To change from Photo to Video mode, press the video button. Go into video mode.
2. Slide up or press the video settings button.
3. Make Video Boost active.
   - By default, Video Boost is configured to 4K resolution, SDR (with 10-bit HDR disabled), and 30 frames per second (FPS) when you first use it. You are free to alter these parameters as you see fit.

- On the top left of the viewfinder, you should see the following icon: This indicates that Video Boost is enabled.
4. Get some footage.
   - Video Boost has a 10-minute maximum recording time. A warning will be shown and recording will be disabled if your storage space is limited.

You'll be offered the option to activate Video Boost and test out Night Sight once the lighting is sufficiently low.

Watch the video and make a copy.

You may immediately view, modify, or share the original video in Google Photos after recording it. The first footage will be in standard dynamic range (1080p) at 30 frames per second.

Press Preview on the Pixel Camera app to see the first clip.

Your video will be automatically backed up and enhanced on the cloud if backup is enabled. If you want to enhance a particular video but don't have backup enabled, you may do it manually.

You won't be able to increase your temporary video until you connect to the internet and save a copy of it.

Check out the enhanced clip

The enhanced video will be prepared and you will get an alert when it's available.

- You need to enable alerts for Google Photos to get them.
- The video's file size and the speed of your internet connection determine how long it will take to upload and process.

To see the original and enhanced versions of a video in Google Photos, just touch on the thumbnails.

- The upgraded video will have this icon.
- If you haven't already, download the enhanced video to your device for optimal playing quality.
- For the greatest viewing experience, the enhanced video will download to your device automatically whenever you're connected to Wi-Fi.

FINDING OUT HOW VIDEO BOOST SAVES FILES

A temporary video file is created whenever you capture video on your phone. To create a boosted video, Video Boost utilizes this file. The scene, resolution, and framerate all have an impact on the final file size.

- You won't lose any cloud storage space in Google Photos since the temporary video file is still being enhanced. The temporary file, however, may eat up space on your phone, which is something you might have noticed.
- After your enhanced video is ready, your phone will immediately remove the temporary file to conserve space.
- Transferring the temporary file from its initial location on your device could prevent automated deletion.

Before your upgraded video replaces the file, you may manually erase it:

1. Launch the Photos app from Google on your mobile device.
2. Open your video library and tap on it.
3. Press the temporary file's thumbnail.
   - Due to its incompatibility, this file cannot be used as the enhanced video.
4. Delete may be found at the bottom.

FIND OUT HOW MUCH DATA IS USED BY VIDEO BOOST

If you've configured backups in Google Photos, Video Boost will use those settings. Video Boost will not enable you to upload or download using your mobile data if you have configured Google Photos to only allow backups while connected to Wi-Fi.

LAUNCH AND EXIT THE GOOGLE CAMERA APP

The most recent Google Camera app is compatible with all Pixel phones.

Android 8.0 and later are required to complete some of these tasks.

LAUNCH GOOGLE CAMERA

There are other methods to open your camera:

- Launch the Google Camera app on your mobile device.
- Hit the Power button on your phone twice.
- Tell it "OK, Google, take a picture." A picture will be captured by your phone after a three-second pause.

GET RID OF THE GOOGLE CAMERA FEATURE

By use of the camera app The Google Camera:

1. Pull up from the bottom, press down, and release.
2. Once you're in the app, swipe up.

Swiping up from the bottom of an earlier Pixel phone's screen may need you to adjust your gesture navigation settings.

USE YOUR PIXEL TO LOCATE, DELETE, OR STORE MEDIA

Using Google Photos on your Pixel phone, you can remove, save, or locate a movie or picture.

REMOVE MEDIA FILES

1. Launch the Google Photos app on your Android device.
2. Access your Google Account by signing in.
3. To delete a whole movie or snapshot, just tap and hold it. Many objects may be selected at once.
4. Tap on Trash Delete located at the top.
   - Any media file you remove from your Google Photos backup will remain in your trash for 60 days.
   - Without a backup, whatever you remove from your Android smartphone will remain in the trash for 60 days.
   - A detachable memory card may contain a picture or video that you believe you have

erased from your Google Photos library. It may be removed using the gallery app on your smartphone.

SAVE MEDIA FILES TO YOUR COMPUTER

1. Launch the Google Photos app on your Android device.
2. Choose a video or picture.
3. To download, press More > Download.

Locate the media you own

Your photographs will be saved on photos.google.com when you enable backup.

Locating your images:

1. Launch the Google Photos module. Photos.
2. Select Photo Album.

SEND AND RECEIVE AUDIO AND TEXT MESSAGES

Use Google Messages to send and receive audio and text messages.

Using Google Messages, you and your friends and contacts may exchange text messages.

Android 6.0 and later are required to complete some of these tasks.

EMBARK ON A DISCUSSION

1. Launch Messages on Google.
2. Hover over Compose.
3. Put the names, numbers, or email addresses of the people you want to send a message to in the "To" field. You have the option to choose either your most recent or whole contact list.

GET IN TOUCH

1. Press on the message field.
2. Tell us what you want. Press Back Back to store it as a draft and return to it later.
3. After finishing, hit the Send button.

COMMUNICATE VIA VOICEMAIL

1. Press on the message field.
2. Hit the microphone button.
3. Transcribe your message.
   - You may preview the voicemail before sending it by saving it as a draft.
   - The send button must be pressed before the voice message may be sent.
4. Select Send.

Decipher transcripts of voice messages

Online transcription becomes enabled with the activation of Live Captions.

With Live Captions off, you may read a transcript of incoming audio messages instead of listening to them.

1. Launch Messages on Google.
2. Launch the conversation from which you got the voicemail.
3. Click on "View transcript" located at the very top of the recorded voice message.

Carry an email.

You can always forward a discussion to a new contact once you've started one.

1. Launch Messages on Google.
2. Join a conversation.
3. You may tap and hold a message.
4. Choose More, and then press Forward.
5. Pick a point of contact.
6. Select Send.

PERUSE INCOMING TEXT CORRESPONDENCE

Just swipe down from the top of your screen and touch on New Message to view a message you just received. Updated message.

Rereading a discussion is as easy as opening it in Google Messages.

- Confirm receipt of all messages: Select all as read by tapping More More.
- Keep a message from being read:

   To indicate a chat as unread in the conversation history, press and hold it.

   To mark an item as unread, go to the top and hit More.

- Launch an audio or video file: Tap on a discussion. Press the Play button next to the recording or video.
- Get in touch with Tap for a discussion. Select "Call Call" from the menu in the upper right.
- Peruse past correspondence: Press More More, followed by Archived, from the list of discussions.

COMMUNICATE WITH MEDIA IN GOOGLE MESSAGES

Communicate with media in Google Messages, including images, videos, and audio.

With Google Messages, you may send and receive multimedia assets including movies, music, GIFs, and images via Multimedia Message Service (MMS).

- Up to Android 6.0, you'll need to follow these instructions.

- Give Google Messages access to transmit and receive files.

FEEL FREE TO SHARE MEDIA FILES, MOVIES, OR GIFS

1. Launch Messages on Google.
2. Gets the ball rolling on a discussion.
3. Use the "Attach" button to include a question.
4. Choose a document.
5. Select Send.

Android Messages do not store any media you capture.

Enhance the quality of your video messages using Google Photos in Google Messages.

- Get the Google Photos app on your device and install it before you begin.
- Please log in to Google Photos before proceeding to Google Messages.

Use Google Messages to share a Google Photos link

- Google Messages can generate a link to your video library if you don't already have it in your Google Photos collection.
- Videos in the shared album may be seen by anybody having the link.

- Videos sent using Google Messages are visible to both you and your spouse when you enable partner sharing.
  1. Launch Messages on Google.
  2. Launch a Text Message or Multimedia Message discussion.
  3. Use the "Attach from Camera or Gallery" button.
  4. Find and choose the video you want to transmit.

     A single link will be generated even if you choose many movies.

  5. Scroll down to "Google Photos link," and then press Include.

     Hit Always to make this the default behavior of sending files as Google Photos links.

  6. Select Send.

     Select Cancel to stop sending the link to Google Messages. Google Photos will continue to receive your video uploads even if Backup & sync is enabled.

     - You can see how big an attachment is before you upload it to Google Photos, regardless of whether the item is already in your library or not.

- While creating, sending, or uploading Google Photos links, you may write and send additional messages.
- Google Photos automatically adds information, such as the video's location, whenever you share a link to it.

See the URLs to your Google Photos

Any link to a Google Photo that you send in a Google Message is viewable.

1. Launch Messages on Google.
2. To access Google Photos, go to the menu bar on the top right, press More Choices, then Settings.
3. Press the Manage links button in Google Photos to see, edit, or remove the links you've shared.

What takes place when you divulge

- When using Google Photos to transmit to a contact:
- The people you shared it with will get two notifications: one from inside the app and another from the developer. Their Sharing page is where you can see the shared item(s).

- You may notify them by email whenever you publish a new album or message to your chat feed.
- Until the user views the album or chat, their profile picture or initials will look faded in the background of the album or conversation.
- Along with the most recent likes, comments, or photographs seen, the activity view will also display their account profile photo or initials when they access the album or chat.
- As soon as they participate in a shared album, like, remark, or upload a photo to a shared album or discussion, their profile picture will transform into their account photo or initial.
- Next to the most recent photographs you've posted to albums or chats, you'll see your account profile photo or initials.
- Some people may be able to slow down their video players to a certain point if you upload a clip that you shot in slow motion.

Fix issues with Google Image connections

- Google Photos and Google Messages are always up-to-date.
- Verify that you have a data or Wi-Fi connection.

- Either make sure your connection is stable or compress the file if the upload is taking too long.
- The receiver will be notified if a video is still in progress when it is sent.

COMMUNICATE VERBALLY

1. Launch Messages on Google.
2. Get the ball rolling on a discussion.
3. Down the microphone button.
4. Tape your message.
5. Select Send.

Sliding left on the chat or closing the message will cancel a voice message.

Describe where you are

1. Launch Messages on Google.
2. Gets the ball rolling on a discussion.
3. Choose "Attach" from the interface. The Chevron Site The Chevron Please transmit.

CONTROL PRIVACY AND SECURITY

Use the Pixel phone's settings to control privacy and security.

By adjusting your privacy and security settings, you can make your phone more secure.

- Android 10 and later are required to complete some of these procedures.
- Touching the screen is necessary for some of these procedures.

OVERSEE YOUR SAFETY CONFIGURATION

1. Go to the Settings app on your phone.
2. Press the lock icon.
3. Your device and Google Account security status will be shown at the top. An alert will show up if you need to do anything crucial to protect your device or accounts.

GET TO KNOW YOUR SECURITY PROFILE

- Found no issues. Your smartphone and Google Account are both completely secure.
- We have security advice that may be implemented to enhance security.
- Safety might be jeopardized: To keep your account or device safe, please read the security advice and implement it.
- Safety is in jeopardy: Your immediate attention is required on some important security matters. To keep your account or device safe, please read the security advice and implement it.

Controllable security configurations

- App safety:

Regularly, Play Protect scans your applications and devices for malicious activity. If any security issues are detected, you will be informed.

- Locate My Item

  Find a way to identify your phone in case it goes missing.

- Critical patch

  You should check whether your system is current.

- Lock screen

  Secure your phone by entering a password, pattern, or PIN.

- Secure unlocking with biometric fingerprint and face recognition

  Unlock your phone and approve transactions using your fingerprint or facial recognition technology.

- Checking Google's security

  See what you've been up to recently, all the devices you've logged into with your Google Account, and the passwords you've stored.

- Version upgrade for Google Play

  Verify whether there are any available updates for your Android OS.

More advanced protection options

- Intelligent Lock

  You may program your smartphone to remain unlocked under certain conditions.

- Apps for managing devices

  Determine which applications have administrative access and delete them.

- SIM card security:

  Use your device only with the correct PIN.

- Credentials and encryption
- Worrying message warnings

  Receive notifications whenever you receive a text message that seems fishy, such as a request, link, or fraud.

- Agents of trust

  Permit your phone to utilize voice matching or Trusted Places as an automated unlock method.

- "Pinning" apps

  By pinning a screen, you may ensure that it remains visible until you remove it.

- Verify the removal of the SIM card

  Be sure you're the one wiping the SIM card before you do it.

- Grants for open-source software

  Find out which open-source licenses for Android are linked to your gadget.

Protection of work profiles

Managing these parameters is also possible with a work profile:

- Make use of a single lock: Put the same passcode on this device as you do on your main account.
- Company profile security: Put a passcode that isn't associated with your account on this gadget.
- Touchless biometric entry in the office: Verify your identity with a fingerprint or face unlock before gaining access to your work profile.

KEEP TRACK OF YOUR PERSONAL INFORMATION

1. Go to the Settings app on your phone.

2. Select Privacy.

Manageable privacy settings

- Privacy Control Panel

  Discover which applications have lately made use of permissions.

- The administrator who grants access

  Manage the data that apps may access.

- Access for cameras

  Make sure no app or service can access your camera.

- Access to microphones

  Make sure no app or service can access your microphone.

- Make passwords visible

  Seeing what you enter might encourage you to choose more complicated and safe passwords.

- Lock screen notifications

  Pick and choose which alerts to display on the lock screen.

- Personal Computer System

  Get personalized recommendations based on your interactions with people, applications, and information.

- Use app data for personalization

  The Android system needs to be able to receive content from applications.

- Make copy and paste easier

  Instruct applications to display a notice whenever they access copied text, pictures, or other material.

- The Google Autofill feature

  Keep track of your stored passwords, addresses, and payment card details.

- Your current Google location

  Keep track of your whereabouts on the move.

- Activation parameters

  Select the actions and data that you would want Google to remember.

You may modify your advertising ID and personalize adverts.

- Diagnostics and use

Contribute data to make Android better.

LOCK THE SCREEN OF YOUR PIXEL PHONE

To make your Android device more secure, you may enable a screen lock. Unlocking your device, often with a PIN, pattern, or password, is required every time you power it on or wake up the screen. You may be able to use your face or fingerprint to unlock some gadgets.

- Android 10 and later are required to complete some of these procedures.
- Touching the screen is necessary for some of these procedures.

PUT A SCREEN LOCK ON OR REMOVE IT

Use a PIN, pattern, or password to encrypt your screen lock and backups, both automatic and manual.

1. Proceed to open the Settings app on your device.
2. Hit the "Security & settings" button.

3. Press the Screen lock to choose a screen lock type.
   - Selecting a new lock requires entering your PIN, pattern, or password if you have already established one.
4. Select the screen lock setting that best suits your needs. Proceed as directed by the on-screen prompts.
5. Next to "Screen lock," touch Settings to see your screen lock's configuration. You may customize the lock screen message, the timing of automated locks, and the locking of the power button.

Lock the screen

Not a lock

- Your phone remains unlocked at all times. It doesn't protect you, but it gets you to the home screen fast.
- Scrub: Use your finger to lightly brush on the screen. It doesn't protect you, but it gets you to the home screen fast.

Regular keyhole

- PIN: Type in four or more digits; however, for extra protection, a six-digit PIN is suggested. Security is often better with longer PINs.

232

- Make a basic design with your finger.
- Please choose a password that consists of at least 4 characters and no underscores. For maximum protection, use a strong password whenever you lock your screen.

Additional secure components

- It is possible to unlock your phone with your fingerprint if your device includes a fingerprint sensor.
- Use Face Unlock to unlock your phone on Pixel 4 and Pixel 7 or later, including Pixel Fold.
- In other situations, including at home, you should leave your device unlocked for a longer period.

By activating the lockdown, you have the option to temporarily disable fingerprint unlocking and Smart Lock.

USE FINGERPRINT AUTHENTICATION TO UNLOCK YOUR PHONE

You can unlock your phone, authenticate purchases, and access some applications using your fingerprint if your smartphone includes a fingerprint sensor— either on the display or the back.

Android 9.0 and later are required to complete some of these tasks.

ARRANGE FOR A FINGERPRINT

For a detailed guide on configuring Fingerprint Unlock, you may use the Pixel phone simulator.

A word of advice: anyone whose fingerprints you link to your account will have full access to your phone and all of your transactions. Anyone else who uses your phone should be able to add their fingerprints to their profile.

Here are the procedures to take for phones running Pixel 6 and later, including Fold:

Access the Settings app on your mobile device.

1. To unlock your device using a fingerprint or face recognition, go to the Security & Privacy menu, then tap Device Lock.
2. Just do what it says on the screen. You will be prompted to set up a secondary PIN, pattern, or password if you haven't done so previously.
3. Quickly scan your first fingerprint.
   - You may find the fingerprint sensor on the underside of your phone's screen. Press down on the fingerprint symbol and hold it there until the sensor lights up and vibrates.

- Maintain a firm pressure with your finger on the screen. Put your middle finger on top of the sensor to begin. To get a good picture of your fingerprint's edges and tips, move your finger in the way suggested.

Here are the steps to take for phones older than the Pixel 5a (5G):

1. Go to the Settings app on your phone.
2. Press the lock icon.
3. To unlock your device using a fingerprint or face recognition, go to the Security & Privacy menu, then tap Device Lock.
4. Just do what it says on the screen. You will be prompted to set up a secondary PIN, pattern, or password if you haven't done so previously.
5. Quickly scan your first fingerprint.
   - Place your index finger on the sensor, not the screen, of your mobile device.
   - Keep your phone in the same hand you use to unlock it. Keep the screen of your phone facing you as an example.

REGARDING THE SAFETY OF FINGERPRINTS

To further secure your phone, we advise you to lock your screen. As an added convenience, your fingerprint sensor can unlock your device.

A couple of factors should be considered, though:

- Compared to a robust PIN, pattern, or password, a fingerprint may not be the most secure option.
- It is possible to unlock your phone using a fingerprint replica. Like many other items you touch, your phone bears the imprint of your fingerprints.
- An additional password, pattern, or PIN will be requested of you. Always have your backup on hand; you could need it in unexpected situations, such as when your phone reboots or when your fingerprint isn't detected.
- Up to five fingerprints may be added.

The location of your fingerprint records

No one else will ever have access to the protected information saved in your fingerprint. Google or any of your phone's applications will not have access to your data.

PUT YOUR FINGERPRINT TO USE

Free your phone

1. To unlock your phone, press and hold the fingerprint sensor located on the back, the screen, or the power button. To wake up the screen on certain phones, you have to touch the power button first.
   - To unlock a phone running Google Pixel 6 or later, press and hold the fingerprint sensor until the screen opens.
2. You may be required to use an alternate PIN, pattern, or password on occasion for security reasons. This must be done following:
   - Even after many attempts, your fingerprint remains unrecognized.
   - Your phone is rebooted.
   - You log in as an alternate user.
   - You haven't been able to unlock using your backup method for over 48 hours.

The fingerprint sensor will become better and better the more you use it; it learns your fingerprint. Your phone securely processes photos of your fingerprints when you use them.

Verify purchases or open applications

Do as instructed when prompted to scan your fingerprint. The app does not get any information about your fingerprints.

CONTROL FINGERPRINT PREFERENCES
Have your fingerprints removed or renamed.

1. Go to the Settings app on your phone.
2. To unlock your device using a fingerprint or face recognition, go to the Security & Privacy menu, then tap Device Lock.
3. Enter your backup screen lock method or scan your current fingerprint.
4. Change it to how you want it.
   - You may remove a fingerprint by tapping the Delete button that appears next to it.
   - Select an existing fingerprint, then touch OK after entering a new name.

Discontinue use and remove fingerprints

Unlock using only a PIN, pattern, or password

Removing your fingerprint will allow you to utilize your secondary PIN or pattern for screen lock:

1. Go to the Settings app on your phone.

2. Press the lock icon.
3. To unlock your device using a fingerprint or face recognition, go to the Security & Privacy menu, then tap Device Lock.
4. Enter your PIN, pattern, password, or scan your fingerprint.
5. Hit the Delete button next to a fingerprint. And so on for every single fingerprint.

You may disable fingerprint unlocking temporarily by activating lockdown.

Disable auto-lock features on mobile devices

If you value your privacy and security, you should keep your screen locked. However, the following alternatives to biometric authentication methods:

1. Go to the Settings app on your phone.
2. To lock the screen, tap on Security.
3. Make a selection or swipe to skip this step. Eliminating fingerprints is the goal here.

USE FACIAL RECOGNITION TO UNLOCK YOUR PHONES

THE MECHANISM OF FACE UNLOCK

With Face Unlock, you can make a personalized model of your face and use it to unlock your Pixel phone. Pixel 4, Pixel 7, and all subsequent Pixel phones, including Pixel Fold, are compatible with Face Unlock. During setup, you'll capture many shots of your face from various angles to generate this face model.

To improve your phone's face recognition in more situations, Face Unlock uses your face photos to update your face model. Your face model is kept safely on your phone and never leaves it, but the photographs of your face that were used to make it aren't. Your phone employs a secure method of processing.

Your face model is only used for Face Unlock when you sign up for the program; it is not shared with any other Google product or service.

Here are the specific steps to take for your Pixel phone model to remove your face model from storage.

- Pixel 7 and subsequent models, along with the Pixel Fold,
- The Nexus 4
- In some areas, facial models might be regarded as biometric data.
- Unintentionally unlocking your phone is as easy as looking at it.
- Compared to a robust PIN, pattern, or password, Face Unlock may not be as safe.
- Someone who has a striking resemblance to you, such as an identical brother, might potentially unlock your phone.
- Also, if someone holds your phone up to your face, they can unlock it. Make sure your phone is always in a secure location, such as your front pocket or purse.
- Facial Unlock may not function properly in low light conditions, whether using sunglasses or a facial covering. For an even smoother unlock experience, we also suggest enrolling in Fingerprint Unlock.

Pixel 7 and subsequent models, as well as the Pixel Fold

You can unlock your phone with Face Unlock if you have a Pixel 7 or later, Pixel phone, or Pixel Fold.

When you log into applications or accept a transaction, you may also use Face Unlock on Pixel 8 and Pixel 8 Pro to verify it's you.

Get Face Unlock Set Up

1. Launch the Settings app on your Pixel phone.
2. Proceed to Device lock by tapping on Security & privacy. From there, choose Face & Fingerprint Unlock.
3. Put in your password, pattern, or PIN.
4. Select Face Unlock and then Get Face Unlock set up.
5. Look over the data shown on the screen.
6. To begin, touch the "I agree" button.
7. Just follow the on-screen prompts.
8. Hit the Finish button.

Modify the face model or toggle face unlock on and off.

The default behavior of Face Unlock may be customized. Both of these options are enabled by default:

- Need eyes to remain open
- Avoid the lock screen

To disable these pre-configured options:

1. Access the Settings app on your mobile device.
2. Access your device by tapping on the "Security & Privacy" icon.
3. Click on Face Unlock after tapping on Face & Fingerprint Unlock.
4. Put in your password, pattern, or PIN.
5. Select Face Unlock.
6. Locate the "When using Face Unlock" section and deselect the desired option.
7. You have to remove your previous face model before you can replace it.

Confirmation is always necessary (Pixel 8 and 8 Pro only).

You have the option to ask for confirmation whenever you use Face Unlock to access applications or authorize a payment.

When using Face Unlock:

1. Access the Settings app on your mobile device.
2. Access your device by tapping on the "Security & Privacy" icon.
3. Click on Face Unlock after tapping on Face & Fingerprint Unlock.
4. Put in your password, pattern, or PIN.
5. Select Face Unlock.

6. Locate the "When using Face Unlock" section and deselect the desired option.

Turn Off or Remove Face Unlock

Repeat steps 1 through 4, and then:

1. To remove a face model, use the Delete button.
2. Get Face Unlock set up.

Make Face Unlock work again

My face keeps being misidentified by Face Unlock.

1. Make sure you've activated biometric authentication by looking at your profile.
   - Launch the Settings app on your Pixel phone.
   - Follow these steps: go to Settings > Security & privacy > Device lock > Face & Fingerprint Unlock > Face Unlock.
   - Put in your password, pattern, or PIN.
2. Make sure you aren't in a completely dark room or anywhere else with very little light.
3. Take off your sunglasses or mask if they're blocking your view of your face, and give it another go.
4. Verify that your default Face Unlock setting is your most common look. Examples include wearing or not wearing a headscarf, spectacles,

or makeup. You have the option to re-enroll your face if there is a substantial change to your look.

Too many times, Face Unlock is activated.

"Tap to check phone" and "Lift to check phone" are both turned on by default. You may disable these features to make it less likely that you will unlock your phone by mistake. Pressing the power button wakes the screen and triggers Face Unlock while these settings are disabled.

There is no way for Face Unlock to activate.

1. "Tap to check phone" and "Lift to check phone" must be enabled for you to use them.
2. To check whether the face is scanning, tap the screen and look for an animated ring or animation around the camera.
3. Make sure the option to unlock with your face and fingerprint is selected:
   - Launch the Settings app on your Pixel phone.
   - Follow these steps: go to Settings > Security & privacy > Device lock > Face & Fingerprint Unlock > Face Unlock.
   - Put in your password, pattern, or PIN.
   - "Face Unlock" appears under "Ways to unlock," with Face added.

- Make sure the unlock feature is enabled on your phone.

The Nexus 4

The Pixel 4 allows you to: Unlock your phone using facial recognition technology.

- Pay the bills.
- Log in to a few applications.

Get Face Unlock Set Up

1. Launch the Settings app on your Pixel phone.
2. Follow these steps: go to Settings > Security & privacy > Device lock > Face & Fingerprint Unlock > Face Unlock.
3. Put in your password, pattern, or PIN.
4. Select Set up Face Unlock toward the bottom of the screen. Then, hit Agree. Finally, tap Start.
5. Squeeze your face into the picture. Gently nudge your nose in the direction of every blue tile.
6. Hit the Finish button.

Customize Face Unlock to your liking

Sign in to applications and confirm payments with your face.

1. Launch the Settings app on your Pixel phone.

2. Follow these steps: go to Settings > Security & privacy > Device lock > Face & Fingerprint Unlock > Face Unlock.
3. Put in your password, pattern, or PIN.
4. App sign-in and payments must be enabled.

If you want to be sure no one else buys anything without your knowledge, you may set it up such that you have to enter your password, pattern, or PIN every time. Choose "Always require confirmation" from the "Requirements for Face Unlock" menu.

Remove all facial data

1. Launch the Settings app on your Pixel phone.
2. Follow these steps: go to Settings > Security & privacy > Device lock > Face & Fingerprint Unlock > Face Unlock.
3. Put in your password, pattern, or PIN.
4. Select Delete face data from the menu at the bottom.

Deactivate Face Unlock.

Open the Settings app on your Pixel phone to enable other methods of unlocking, such as PIN, pattern, or password, in addition to Face Unlock.

1. Follow these steps: go to Settings > Security & privacy > Device lock > Face & Fingerprint Unlock > Face Unlock.
2. Put in your password, pattern, or PIN.
3. Under "Use Face Unlock," disable the feature that unlocks your phone.

If you disable "Unlocking your phone," Face Unlock will continue to work for app logins and payment completion. You may disable facial Unlock entirely by erasing your facial data.

Need eyes to remain open

You have the option to have Face Unlock requires that your eyes be open to prevent your phone from unlocking while they are closed.

1. When using Face Unlock:
2. Launch the Settings app on your Pixel phone.
3. Follow these steps: go to Settings > Security & privacy > Device lock > Face & Fingerprint Unlock > Face Unlock.
4. Put in your password, pattern, or PIN.

Select "Require eyes to be open" from the "Requirements for Face Unlock" menu.

Make Face Unlock work again

My setup is a mess.

- Try setting up Face Unlock while dressed normally and in an environment where you normally use your phone. Put your spectacles or headscarf on before you arrive at work if you wear them daily.
- You can still set up with restricted mobility if you have trouble moving your head. Press Setup to begin configuring Face Unlock for restricted vision or head movement.
- Verify that there is enough light where you are.

Face Unlock is not working for me.

Your phone may not always allow you to unlock it with your face because of extra security measures. Unlocking your phone is still possible:

- To unlock your phone, swipe up from the screen.
- Put in your password, pattern, or PIN.

When Face Unlock fails frequently on your phone:

- Those who hide their faces with masks or dark sunglasses should remove them.
- You should seek a well-lit area if you find yourself in a dimly lit one.

- Seek shelter from the sun if you find yourself in a sunny area.
- Keep your phone at a 45-degree angle and hold it upright in front of your face.
- To clean the surface of your screen, use a gentle, dry towel.
- You will need to reset Face Unlock and remove your face data if you decide to alter your look.

SET THE DURATION FOR WHICH YOUR PHONE MAY REMAIN UNLOCKED

For example, if you routinely carry your Pixel phone in your pocket or have it synced with another device you use often, you have the option to keep it unlocked. With Extend Unlock, you'll only have to enter your PIN, pattern, or password once to unlock. It all comes down to the gadget you're using.

- Android 10 and later are required to complete some of these procedures.
- Touching the screen is necessary for some of these procedures.

Refrain from locking your phone

1. Install a screen lock to protect your device.
2. Launch the Settings app on your smartphone.

3. After that, choose "Security & privacy." Continue with Extend Unlock for even more privacy and security.
4. Put in your password, pattern, or PIN.
5. Just choose a choice and follow the instructions that pop up.

Your lock screen will show the Unlock icon while Extend Unlock is activated and switched on. If you use Extend Unlock, your smartphone will remain unlocked for a maximum of four hours.

Once again, to secure your device:

1. Make sure you press both the Power and Volume up keys simultaneously.
2. Press the "Lockdown" button.

Disable Extend Unlock

1. Launch the Settings app on your smartphone.
2. After that, choose "Security & privacy." Continue with Extend Unlock for even more privacy and security.
3. Put in your password, pattern, or PIN.
4. Select "On-body detection".
5. Switch off the feature that detects when a person is on their body.

6. Take away any trusted gadgets and locations. + if desired.

Master the art of locking

When you have Extend Unlock enabled, lock your phone.

Secure the area

1. Make sure you press both the Power and Volume up keys simultaneously.
2. On the lockdown screen, tap the button.

The ability to remotely lock a device via Locate My Item

Locking your device is as easy as using your computer, tablet, or other mobile device.

Never lock your phone while it's in your possession.

Activate or deactivate on-body detection.

1. Launch the Settings app on your smartphone.
2. Next, choose "Security & privacy." Additional protection and privacy, followed by On-body detection and Extended Unlock.
3. Toggle the switch for Use On-body detection.

Detection Methods Used on the Body

- Your unlocked device will remain unlocked for as long as it detects your body. For devices that can automatically lock themselves, such as when placed on a table, this process can take up to one minute.
- Your device may take 5-10 minutes to lock after getting into a vehicle, whether it's a car, bus, train, or something else entirely.

   Your device may not be able to lock automatically while you are on a boat or airplane. If necessary, lock manually.

You can tell when you're carrying your device by looking at the accelerometer data it stores about your walking pattern. This information is erased from your device once you disable on-body detection.

When you're in a safe location, don't lock your phone.

Utilize reputable sources

- Give your gadget permission to use your precise location.

Tip: Wi-Fi is optimal for trusted locations.

The place you trust is only an approximation.

Your reliable spot doesn't have to be limited to your house or personal space. As far as 100 meters away, it may keep your phone unlocked.

Copying or manipulating location signals is possible. Someone may potentially open your device if they have access to certain tools.

Take alerts from your lock screen.

Secure the area

Lockdown will remain active until you open your device, so please be aware of this. Each time you want to use lockdown, you must activate it.

1. Make sure you press both the Power and Volume up keys simultaneously.
2. On the lockdown screen, tap the button. Within the confines of your lock screen, this toggles off all alerts, fingerprint unlocking, and Extend Unlock.

While linked to a reliable device, leave your device unlocked.

Include a reliable Bluetooth accessory

Turn on Bluetooth on your mobile device. Get the hang of activating Bluetooth.

1. Launch the Settings app on your smartphone.
2. Next, choose "Security & privacy." Follow that with Extend Unlock for further privacy and security.
3. After that, tap on Trusted Devices. Include a reliable gadget.
4. Select a device from the list.
- By linking your mobile device to a reliable device, such as a Bluetooth watch or vehicle speaker system, you may extend the amount of time that your device can remain open. We advise staying away from Bluetooth keyboards and cases since they are always in the vicinity of your mobile device.
5. Not required: Simply tapping on the Bluetooth device you want to delete will do the trick. Hit Remove thereafter.
6. Get your phone unlocked. It will remain unlocked as long as it is linked to the trusted device.

Stick to Bluetooth devices you know and trust.

An imposter may theoretically keep your smartphone unlocked by pretending to be your Bluetooth partner.

If your device alerts you: If your device detects that you aren't connected to a secure network, it will alert you. Unlocking your smartphone may be necessary.

Different Bluetooth devices have different possible ranges of connection. Factors such as your device's model, the Bluetooth device, and the surrounding environment determine the range. The maximum range for Bluetooth is 100 meters. Someone might potentially get access to your smartphone if they manage to steal it when it is close to your trusted device and your trusted device has already unlocked it.

HAVE THE PLAN TO RECOVER A MISPLACED PIXEL PHONE

Be ready in case you misplace your phone by making sure Find My Device can locate it.

Some procedures need Android 8.0 or later.

Verify that your gadget can be located

To identify an Android device, you must ensure that:

- Is currently logged onto their Google Account
- Is Location enabled?
- Checked the "Find My Device" box

- Powered up and linked to a mobile data or WiFi network.
- You can still access your device's most recent location even when it's turned off or not connected to mobile data or WiFi, as long as you've selected "Store recent location."
- Can be found on the Google Play Store

For Android devices to be able to lock or wipe data, you must ensure that:

- Possesses authority
- Uses cellular data or WiFi when linked
- Is logged onto Google with an active Google Account enabled with Find My Device
- Can be found on the Google Play Store

Make sure you're logged into your Google Account.

- Launch the Settings app on your smartphone.
- Select your profile picture by tapping on it in the upper right corners.
- If you signed in using an email address, make sure it's valid.

Verify that the Venue is set to

1. Launch the Settings app on your smartphone.

2. Press on the Place.
3. Open the Location app.

If you hide a device on Google Play, it will not be visible in Find My Device. So, make sure that Find My Device is turned on.

1. Launch the Settings app on your smartphone.
2. Select File > Security > Find My Device.
3. For those who don't see "Security," try selecting "Security & location" or "Google And then Security."
4. You should make sure that "Find My Device" is enabled.

Verify that your gadget can be located

Google Play's hidden devices will not be visible in Find My Device.

1. Verify that the "Show In Menus" checkbox is marked at the upper left.

Launch the program

Installing the Find My Device software on one Android device will make it possible to use it to locate another.

Made in the USA
Monee, IL
30 January 2024